D1086368

The Mind of the African Strongman

ADST-DACOR Diplomats and Diplomacy Series

Series Editor: Margery Boichel Thompson

Since 1776, extraordinary men and women have represented the United States abroad under widely varying circumstances. What they did and how and why they did it remain little known to their compatriots. In 1995, the Association for Diplomatic Studies and Training (ADST) and DACOR, an organization of foreign affairs professionals, created the Diplomats and Diplomacy book series to increase public knowledge and appreciation of the professionalism of American diplomats and their involvement in world history. Hank Cohen's portraits of African leaders he has encountered in his long diplomatic career is the 57th volume in the series.

RELATED TITLES IN ADST SERIES

Claudia E. Anyaso, *Fifty Years of U.S. Africa Policy: Reflections of Assistant Secretaries for African Affairs and U.S. Embassy Officials*

Gordon S. Brown, *Toussaint's Clause: The Founding Fathers and the Haitian Revolution*

Thompson Buchanan, *Mossy Memoir of a Rolling Stone*

Herman J. Cohen, *Intervening in Africa: Superpower Peacemaking in a Troubled Continent*

Donald P. Gregg, *Pot Shards: Fragments of a Life Lived in CIA, the White House, and the Two Koreas*

Robert E. Gribbin, *In the Aftermath of Genocide: The U.S. Role in Rwanda*

Brandon Grove, *Behind Embassy Walls: The Life and Times of an American Diplomat*

Michael P. E. Hoyt, *Captive in the Congo: A Consul's Return to the Heart of Darkness*

Edmund J. Hull, *High-Value Target: Countering al Qaeda in Yemen*

Cameron Hume, *Mission to Algiers: Diplomacy by Engagement*

Dennis C. Jett, *American Ambassadors: The Past, Present, and Future of America's Diplomats*

Robert H. Miller, *Vietnam and Beyond: A Diplomat's Cold War Education*

David D. Newsom, *Witness to a Changing World*

Richard B. Parker, *Uncle Sam in Barbary: A Diplomatic History*

———, *Memoirs of a Foreign Service Arabist*

Howard B. Schaffer, *Ellsworth Bunker: Global Troubleshooter, Vietnam Hawk*

Raymond F. Smith, *The Craft of Political Analysis for Diplomats*

James W. Spain, *In Those Days: A Diplomat Remembers*

William G. Thom, *African Wars: Recollections of a Defense Intelligence Officer*

Jean Wilkowski, *Abroad for Her Country: Tales of a Pioneer Woman Ambassador in the U.S. Foreign Service*

For a complete list of series titles, visit <adst.org/publications>

THE MIND OF THE AFRICAN STRONGMAN

Conversations with Dictators, Statesmen, and Father Figures

HERMAN J. COHEN

An ADST-DACOR Diplomats and Diplomacy Book

Washington, DC

Copyright © 2015 by Herman J. Cohen

New Academia Publishing 2015

The views and opinions in this book are solely those of the author and not necessarily those of the Association for Diplomatic Studies and Training, DACOR, Inc., or the Government of the United States.

All rights reserved. No part of this book may be reproduced or transmitted in any form or by any means, electronic or mechanical, including photocopying, recording, or by any information storage and retrieval system.

Indexing by Amron Gravett, Wild Clover Book Services.

Printed in the United States of America.

Library of Congress Control Number: 2015933925
ISBN 978-0-9864353-0-0 paperback (alk. paper)
ISBN 978-0-9864353-1-7 hardcover (alk. paper)

An imprint of New Academia Publishing

New Academia Publishing
PO Box 27420, Washington, DC 20038-7420
info@newacademia.com - www.newacademia.com

To Suzanne, Marc, and Alain

Contents

Introduction

After fifty years of postcolonial independence, why are fifty African nations doing relatively poorly in terms of socioeconomic development as of the beginning of 2015? Why does Africa control less than two percent of world trade? Why do poverty levels continue to be high despite high GDP growth rates based on strong world commodity prices? Why do internal conflicts continue to cause havoc in countries with major resources and strong growth potential, such as the Democratic Republic of the Congo, the Sudan, the Federal Republic of Nigeria, and the Republic of Mali? Why are relatively young African multiparty democracies so fragile?

After more than a half century of independence, the argument that African nations are suffering from continued colonial exploitation rings hollow. Multinational corporations are busy in many African countries extracting oil and minerals for worldwide export. Some African intellectuals say that these corporations do little for African development. On the other hand, international observers criticize African governments for inept, or even corrupt, management of the significant taxes and royalties that come from these extractive industries. They ask why the revenue from resources does not go toward infrastructure improvement or rural development.

Nonetheless, some African countries are starting to move ahead. Ironically, these countries tend to be smaller and with fewer natural resources. Kenya, Mozambique, Tanzania, and Senegal are making up for a lack of resources with smart governance and good management, as well as with steadily improving democracy. The biggest and most resource-rich countries, especially Nigeria, Democratic Republic of Congo, and the Sudan, are all doing very poorly.

Are the barriers to progress essentially cultural? Are they geographic, ethnic, or political factors, or basically the result of inept leadership? Intimate conversations with some of the first leaders of postcolonial African countries provide some explanations as to Africa's serious problems in a globalized environment. Will it be possible for the second and third generations of African leaders to learn from the experiences of their founding fathers, or will they remain prisoners of African history and culture?

Since 1990, there has been a growing body of scholarship supporting the concept that economic progress within the emerging nations is a function of culture.[1] Flash back to the 1950s when most of sub-Saharan Africa was still under European colonial rule. Countries like Nigeria, Ghana, Kenya, Côte d'Ivoire, Guinea, Congo, and Madagascar had higher GNP per capita than Southeast Asian countries like Malaysia, Hong Kong, Korea, and Indonesia. By the year 1990 the situation was totally reversed. The Southeast Asians had moved significantly ahead of the Africans, having taken away Africa's market share for products like palm oil, coffee, sugar, and cassava starch. As of the year 2015 not a single sub-Saharan nation could be described as having moved into the high-growth status necessary for achieving economic "takeoff."

By listening to the words of African leaders, we can get a glimpse of why they and their political elites have not created the necessary institutions and enabling environment needed to encourage the type of investments necessary for sustainable growth. Between 1975 and 1995, the World Bank assisted the majority of African countries in their efforts to avoid economic collapse. Their economic reform programs were given the name "structural adjustment." The purpose was to establish basic economic policies that could reverse years of minus five percent growth toward positive five percent growth. On the whole, these programs achieved their goals. But it has since been difficult for the African states to move from modest growth to the type of growth necessary to make the great leap toward rapid and sustainable movement into middle-income status.

More and more African intellectuals are looking at cultural norms to explain the lack of real movement toward economic modernization. In Southeast Asian countries, for example, the private entrepreneur is usually considered an economic development partner to the political leadership. In Africa, the private entrepreneur who is not directly linked to the ruling political party is usually considered a threat to power. That is why Africans hold so much of their money outside of Africa rather than invest it at home.[2]

Listening to Africa's founding fathers, as I have over thirty-eight years, the dominant message is clear. "Our peoples are immature. They are not ready to be given responsibility for our nations' economic progress. We need to provide close guidance and exercise control." In short, sub-Saharan Africa has been, and to a great extent continues to be, a prisoner of its cultural history.

Notes

1. David S. Landes, *The Wealth and Poverty of Nations: Why Some Are So Rich and Others So Poor* (New York: W.W. Norton, 1998).
2. Daniel Etounga-Manguelle, "Does Africa Need a Cultural Adjustment Program?" in Lawrence Harrison and Samuel Huntington, eds., *Culture Matters: How Values Shape Human Progress* (New York: Basic Books 2000), p. 65.

GROUP I

The Francophones:
France's Anchors in Africa

The late president of the Republic of Senegal, Léopold Sédar Senghor (right), and the U.S. ambassador to Dakar, Herman J. Cohen, at a reception for a visiting head of state in Dakar in March 1978.
Credit: USIS Dakar

CHAPTER 1

Léopold Sédar Senghor—Senegal

Poet, Scholar, Statesman, and
Subtle Political Strongman

Historical Note

Léopold Senghor was born in 1906 into a modest Roman Catholic family on the Atlantic Coast about eighty miles south of Dakar, the capital city of Senegal and the headquarters of French colonialism in West Africa. A senior French colonial administrator was impressed by Léopold's intelligence and proposed to take charge of his education. The family agreed. This led to Léopold's completing secondary school at an elite establishment in Dakar and going on to higher studies in France. He graduated from the prestigious École Normale Supérieur in Paris shortly before the onset of the Second World War, earning a doctorate in grammar. He served in the French army during the war.

After the war, he returned to Senegal and plunged into politics and the movement to gain independence from France. He was close to the French Socialist Party. When France granted self-government in 1958, he became Senegal's first president. Before final independence, Senegal and the French Soudan agreed to form a federation to be called Mali. The federation was dissolved shortly after it was established because of a disagreement as to who would be president. The Senegalese said that the president had to be Senghor, and the Soudanese said it had to be Modibo Keita.

After full independence in 1961, Senghor had to use force to get rid of his prime minister, who was trying to act independently. During these early years, Senghor demonstrated an iron will and a willingness to use violence if necessary to maintain his power.

After 1964, his authority was uncontested. Senghor was elected president despite being a Roman Catholic in a country that is 95 percent Muslim.

Senghor remained president until 1980, when he retired voluntarily. During his tenure, he was widely known on the international stage as a moderate African statesman and a champion of "negritude," in support of the dignity of people of African descent anywhere in the world. He was also a successful poet and a scholar of African history and culture. His two decades in office were marked by the consolidation of Senegalese nationalism, patriotism, and cultural pride.

Despite its small size and lack of resources, Senegal was considered one of the leading nations of independent Africa, and Senghor was considered one of its most influential leaders. Nevertheless, during his tenure little was accomplished toward economic development, and poverty deepened. While Senghor founded a culturally proud nation called Senegal, he failed to identify solutions to the country's most profound problems.

❖ ❖ ❖

The Republic of Senegal's first president, Léopold Sédar Senghor, had a direct impact on me even before I met him. In August 1977, I was in Washington, D.C., preparing for my assignment to Dakar, Senegal, as the US ambassador. I was then completing a three-year tour in Paris as the embassy political counselor.

The embassy in Dakar informed me that I needed to wear a morning outfit to present my credentials to President Senghor during a formal ceremony. I went to a downtown Washington establishment that specialized in formal wear. When I told them that I wanted to purchase a morning coat and striped trousers, they expressed astonishment. The salesperson said, "We sell one of these about once every three or four years to the new solicitor general, who wears it when trying a case before the Supreme Court. Otherwise, we deal only in rentals for special occasions." So, before I even arrived in Dakar, I knew that I would be dealing with a stickler for traditional European-style protocol.

The presentation of credentials ceremony took place in

September 1977 at the presidential palace. The formal part was a public exchange of remarks during which the president and I made commitments to continue a constructive dialogue between our two friendly governments. The really interesting part was a one-on-one conversation in the president's private office, where I learned that Senghor was a kind and considerate person, at least to foreign dignitaries.

After reviewing bilateral relations, Senghor lowered his voice and asked, "Mr. Ambassador, from your name, I assume that you are of the Jewish faith. Is that correct?" I nodded affirmatively. "I want to assure you," he continued,

> that while Senegal is 95 percent Muslim, there is no danger to you or your family. I myself am a devout Catholic, and there was no religious opposition to my being elected Senegal's first president. We are a very tolerant people. We celebrate Christian holidays, and many families are mixed.
>
> In terms of Senegal's foreign relations, we acceded to Egypt's request to break diplomatic relations with Israel after the 1973 Sinai war. But we continue to have friendly contacts with Israel. Shimon Peres comes to visit about three times a year, and we meet with the Israeli delegation to the annual meeting of Socialist International.
>
> Also, Mr. Ambassador, I want you to know that there is Jewish blood in my very own family. My first wife was the daughter of Félix Eboué, the Martinique-born governor of the French African colony of Chad during World War II and a De Gaulle loyalist. Eboué's wife was a Jewish lady from Paris. Therefore, his children were half-Jewish. Consequently, my two sons with Eboué's daughter have Jewish blood.

After being reassured about security, I settled down to the regular business of diplomatic relations. There was an office of the Palestine Liberation Organization in Dakar, and we were experiencing a high degree of Palestinian terrorism internationally. My embassy security officer insisted on my taking varying random routes to the office every day, and my two sons did the same traveling to and from school.

During my periodic talks with Senghor, always one-on-one, I found him to be highly interested and well informed in world affairs. Although socialist in his politics, he was under no illusions about the Soviet Union. He belonged to the nonaligned movement but was totally pro-West in his sentiments, just like the French Socialist Party. Today, as we view with alarm events in nuclear-armed Pakistan, I remember Senghor telling me back in 1978 that Pakistan was "dangerous and obscurantist."

Senghor also believed that he had ideas to contribute to the search for peace and security in the world. After the Camp David agreement between Israel and Egypt in 1978, hosted by President Jimmy Carter, Senghor did everything possible to prevent the Islamic countries from punishing Egypt. I spent many hours with him and the Egyptian ambassador developing strategies for meetings of the Organization of Islamic States.

Like most heads of state, Senghor had a strong ego. It comes with the territory. In mid-1978, about six weeks had gone by without my seeing Senghor. I never asked to see him unless I had something serious to discuss. During this slack period, I received a call from Senghor's secretary. "Mr. Ambassador, the president would like to see you. Would tomorrow at 4 p.m. be convenient?"

Needless to say, I accepted. Senghor's first remark at that meeting was, "Mr. Ambassador, I have not seen you for a long time. I do not want too much time to go by without Washington knowing my views." He then proceeded to expound about the Middle East. He was especially interested in demolishing the idea that the occupied Palestinian territories be amalgamated with Jordan to form a true Palestinian state.

One of Senghor's highest priorities was the concept of negritude. A senior colonial official visiting his village had identified his high intelligence as a child and recommended to his parents that he be educated in an elite Catholic school in Dakar, where he saw his first electric light bulb. During his university years in France, he met with other black intellectuals from Africa and the French Caribbean territories, including the novelist-philosopher Franz Fanon, who had a strong influence on Senghor's development. During this period, he and his friends developed the concept of negritude. The idea was that people of African descent had the same potential for intellectual development as everyone else and that potential should be nurtured. The concept went hand in hand with the anti-colonial movement in Africa.

During his presidency, Senghor continued to write and act with the concept of negritude in mind. There were two examples that I encountered directly.

First, Senghor considered the people of Indonesian and Australian New Guinea to be of African descent. He therefore supported independence for these two territories. Australian New Guinea became independent as Papua New Guinea. But Indonesia refused to consider independence for the other half of New Guinea, known as West Irian. A West Irian nationalist movement existed, and Senghor invited them to set up an office in Dakar, with Senegalese financing. In 1978, the Islamic Conference, a multinational grouping with a secretariat in Saudi Arabia, decided to have its annual meeting in Dakar. Indonesia threatened to boycott the meeting because of the West Irian independence office. Senghor solved the immediate problem by sending the West Irian nationalists to Europe for the duration of the meeting, but he did not abandon his support.

The second example was in Angola, the oil-rich former Portuguese colony in southwest Africa. Portugal gave independence to Angola in 1974 with absolutely no preparation. Former anti-Portuguese insurgent movements started fighting each other after the Portuguese departed. Thanks to Cuban assistance, the Marxist insurgent movement, MPLA, gained power in the capital city, but guerilla warfare continued in the countryside. The main anti-MPLA fighting group was called UNITA, under the leadership of a charismatic intellectual named Jonas Savimbi, who claimed to be pro-West and anti-communist. Almost all African governments recognized the MPLA government. Senghor, however, financed a UNITA office in Dakar. When I asked him why he did this, his reply was based on negritude. He said that the leaders of the MPLA government were all people of mixed African and Portuguese blood who did not speak African languages. Savimbi and his UNITA movement were pure Africans, representing the African majority.

In France, Senghor had attended the prestigious École Normale Supérieur, which has a highly competitive entrance examination. It prepares future college and high school professors, many of whom go on to distinguished careers in government and the private sector. French president Pompidou was Senghor's contemporary at the school. Senghor majored in grammar, and was fascinated with words and languages as a result. In the context of negritude, Senghor liked to examine the languages of black people in the Western world. He was also an accomplished poet, who won several prizes that led to his induction into the super-prestigious French Academy.

In one conversation, Senghor told me that he was studying the "jazz" language of New Orleans to determine if there were links to West Africa. He said that one of his discoveries was in the jazz term "I dig you." He said that in the Senegalese language, Wolof, a person listening to an explanation or instruction expresses his understanding by repeatedly saying "deugela," pronounced "diggala," with the emphasis on "dig."

Of greater significance, Senghor believed strongly that Western civilization had its beginnings among the Nubians of the Nile, who, he argued, were Africans. The Nubians were at the heart of the Egyptian civilization that constituted the bedrock of Western civilization, he claimed. Some scholars agree with his claim for the Nubians but do not necessarily consider them to be authentic Africans.

As a Catholic with deep respect for the Muslim religion as practiced by the Senegalese people for many centuries, Senghor went out of his way to maintain good relations with the leading clerics of the different Muslim brotherhoods. Nonetheless, I had the feeling that he liked to tease them from time to time.

Every year, on the anniversary of Senegalese independence, Senghor held a large formal reception at the presidential palace. The ladies wore their best Parisian gowns, and the men wore either traditional dress or black tie. At one of the receptions, my wife and I arrived early. So, we decided to stand in front of the main entrance to enjoy the arrival of the other guests and admire their finery. The ambassador of Saudi Arabia joined us, wearing his finest Arab robes and headdress. As we watched the elegant Senegalese ladies sporting their very feminine fashions, and very little modesty, I turned to the Saudi envoy and asked, "Mr. Ambassador, what do you think about these Muslim ladies and their high fashion?' The

Saudi ambassador responded formally, "I consider them to be true believers." That put me in my place.

Senghor also used the judicial system to wear down some of the Muslim social practices, such as polygamy and easy divorces for the males. He instituted a law that required couples about to marry to decide whether the marriage will be monogamous or polygamous, and not to be changed later. He also enacted legislation that established alimony to be paid by the man to his divorced wife. This caused such consternation among the Muslim men that some decided to quit working in order not to have resources that could be confiscated through alimony.

Senghor was a man of principle. In 1979, the Soviets invaded Afghanistan, causing President Jimmy Carter great angst. Carter decided to promote a boycott of the 1980 Olympic games in Moscow. Shortly after the invasion, Senghor traveled to the United States to accept an honorary degree at Bridgeport University in Connecticut. He invited me to ride in his presidential aircraft. President Carter invited him to the Oval Office for an informal chat. Carter decided to make a strong pitch to Senghor to lead an African boycott of the Moscow Olympics. Senghor said he could not do that. He explained that in 1976, the Africans called for a boycott of the Olympic games in Montreal as a protest against Western inaction against apartheid in South Africa and illegal white minority rule in Southern Rhodesia. The American government at the time opposed the boycott on the grounds that politics should not be interjected into the Olympic event. So, the Africans would now follow the earlier American admonition. Senghor was adamant and did not budge.

President Carter did not easily give up on his quest for a Moscow boycott. He asked world heavyweight boxing champion Mohammed Ali to travel to African countries to plead for a boycott in late 1979. Senegal was the last stop on an eight-country tour. Senghor decided not to have anything formal for Ali's visit, in contrast to his usual treatment of foreign presidential delegations. Instead, it would be a festive occasion, with maximum exposure of Ali to the Senegalese population.

One of the events involved Ali kissing and blessing Senegalese children named after him. Ali sat in my living room kissing the children, whose mothers formed a long line down the street.

Afterward, he went to the boxing matches that are a popular sport in Senegal, distributing hundred dollar bills to handicapped persons lining his path. He was invited to enter the ring and put on gloves. After a short period of sparring, Ali allowed himself to be "knocked out" by his Senegalese opponent. My wife Suzanne still tells the story of Ali emptying our refrigerator nonstop between events.

Senghor decided to deal with Ali's official business regarding the boycott at his country beach house about fifty miles south of Dakar. He invited Ali to lunch along with young people from his and neighboring families.

My wife and I arrived at Senghor's house about a half hour early in accordance with protocol, since we represented President Carter for this "official visit." Senghor took us around to shake hands with every one of the Senegalese employees at the house. When that was done, Senghor pointed out that all of the employees came from the Peul ethnic group. This is an ethnic group of nomadic heritage living in several West African countries. In Nigeria, for example they are called Fulani. In Mauritania they are called Halpulaar.

Senghor then explained why there was no diversity in his household staff. He said that he considered the Peul to be the most intelligent of the various ethnic groups in West Africa. With increased experience in West Africa after our stay in Senegal, we had extensive contacts with Peul intellectuals and officials and found among them a great desire for education and intellectual accomplishment.

It was a most enjoyable lunch, with Senghor explaining to Mohammed Ali why he could not join in the boycott, and Ali expressing understanding. Toward the end of the lunch, Senghor whispered in Ali's ear, and they both left the room together. After about twenty minutes, they both returned. The final event was an exchange of toasts. Senghor toasted the excellent relations between Senegal and the United States. Ali decided to toast Senghor personally. Ali said that the visit to Senegal was absolutely the best of all his visits in Africa. He expressed particular awe at the fact that the president of Senegal personally showed him the way to the bathroom and waited for him to finish and escort him back to the other guests.

Another American official visitor who amused Senghor was Ms. Lillian Carter, the president's mother, who made an official goodwill visit to several West African countries, including Senegal.

At a private dinner, Ms. Lillian regaled Senghor with stories about politics in Plains, Georgia. But the most memorable story involved Ms. Lillian's service in the Peace Corps in India at the age of 62. She spoke of an article in an Atlanta newspaper that said, "Mrs. Lillian Carter, Georgia Governor Jimmy Carter's mother, is in Bombay, India, giving out free condoms." Ms. Lillian acknowledged that she was working on family planning in Bombay. She told Senghor that while she was promoting lower birth rates in India, her children in Georgia "were doing just the opposite."

Mrs. Carter also described her official visit to the Gambia, Senegal's intertwined neighbor. She asked Senghor why the Muslim Gambian president's wife at the first night's dinner was not the same lady as the president's wife at the second night's dinner? She also showed off the heavy gold bracelet that she received as a gift from the president of the Gambia.

She turned to me and asked, "Mr. Ambassador, how much is this worth?"

Without blinking an eye, I said, "Ms. Lillian, this bracelet is worth $99.99. Since it is one cent below the official US government limit for accepting gifts, you can keep it."

She turned to Senghor and said, "Mr. President, if I keep this bracelet worth thousands of dollars, my son will be insulted in every newspaper in the United States."

After an hour of listening to Carter family anecdotes, Senghor said, "Madame Carter, you should write a book."

Senghor was so taken by Lillian Carter that he talked to her about a subject that is not often discussed between Senegalese and outsiders. This was the subject of caste in Senegalese society. Very much like India, West African cultures have caste systems that rigidly separate various segments of the population. Until the end of the twentieth century, marriages between castes were discouraged within families, and the lower castes tended to be victims of discrimination. A common insult-joke among intellectuals during my time in Senegal was, "Stop disagreeing with me. You are my slave."

Senghor told Mrs. Carter that he could never speak about caste in public, but he was doing everything possible to uplift the lower castes. That was why intellectuals named Thiam from a lower caste grouping were editor-in-chief of the most important daily newspaper and prime minister of the government.

Senghor saw the Senegalese people, who tended to give their first loyalty to their Muslim brotherhoods, their ethnic families, and their tribal elders, as being unready for democracy. He therefore kept politics under tight control. He decreed that Senegal would have three political parties. His Socialist Party was in the center. He allowed the creation of a right-wing "Liberal" party (i.e., pro-capitalist) and a left-wing revolutionary party in the image of the Communist party of the Soviet Union.

Elections were rigged until Senghor's handpicked successor, Abdou Diouf, allowed a fair count and was defeated for reelection in 2000 by the right-wing leader Abdoulaye Wade. Although Senghor and his family were not corrupt, the ruling Socialist Party was efficient in stealing public revenues for patronage purposes.

Senghor could be quite arbitrary in selective cases. He banned a film directed by Ousmane Sembene, one of Africa's legendary cinema artists, because he considered it insulting to the ruling elites. And when it came to the economy, Senghor was a true French socialist. He nationalized the commanding heights of the economy when he came to power in 1960, causing Senegal to suffer greatly from negative economic growth for years. During Senghor's time in office, there were virtually no free and independent media except for a couple of weekly satirical sheets. There was a government-financed newspaper, as well as government-controlled radio and TV stations.

Senghor was not unfamiliar with Senegal's impoverished interior. He had his roots there. He knew what was going on. He once gave me a ten-minute lecture on the devastation to the environment caused by goats. Nevertheless, I am sure that I traveled to Senegal's interior far more than he did. We had a hundred Peace Corps volunteers working in Senegalese villages. I made a practice of trying to visit as many of them as possible, thereby learning about the political economy of the heart of the nation.

I found that Senegal's rural populations were stagnating. I saw very few medical facilities and very little infrastructure maintenance. In addition, I saw brewing ethnic trouble in Senegal's far south, in the Casamance region. There, I saw Muslim livestock farmers moving down from the north with their flocks, seeking to escape chronic drought in the north. They were moving in on a mixed population of sedentary farmers, with a large percentage of resentful Christians. The situation was explosive, but I saw no attention being paid to it in Dakar. A few years later, the long Casamance insurgency began, and it was still spreading violence three decades later. Fortunately for him, Senghor was living in retirement when the war began and did not have to deal with it.

In the far north, on the Senegal River, I saw trouble brewing on the border with the Islamic Republic of Mauritania, whose population is two-thirds Arab and one-third African. The Africans live mainly in the far south of the country near the north bank of the river. During Senghor's time, the African population of Mauritania was far more advanced culturally than the majority Arab population, which was just emerging from centuries of nomadic life and a history of slave ownership. The African population had its roots in Senegal south of the river and was able to obtain arms and support from its ethnic brothers. A decade after Senghor's retirement, the border erupted with mass expulsions from both sides and refugees piled up on both sides. As assistant secretary of state in 1989, I traveled to both countries and worked out a border settlement, but the bitterness remained. Again, it was an embryonic problem that diplomats saw long before the government in Dakar.

Because of a historical colonial error, Senegal is virtually bisected by the former British colony of The Gambia. Movement of people and goods between north and south Senegal has to traverse The Gambia across the River Gambia . There is no bridge. There are two ferry services, in the center and near the Atlantic coast. The center ferry service, at the Gambian town of Farafenni, is extremely slow. Trucks are frequently kept waiting for up to four days to cross. The expenses are high. The Senegalese population south of the river, in Casamance, feels alienated from, and neglected by, the central government in Dakar.

In 1978, the European Union offered to finance the construction of a toll bridge across the river at Farafenni. The Government of The Gambia insisted that the bridge should be part of a dam that would serve to block the intrusion of seawater during the low water season. Because the European Union saw no need for the much more expensive dam, the request was refused, and the bridge was not built. This infuriated President Senghor, who was counting on the construction of the bridge to bring the people of the Casamance closer to the rest of Senegal, thereby ameliorating their sense of neglect.

Shortly after the decision not to have a bridge over the River Gambia, I spoke to Senghor on another matter. He was still fuming over the decision. I said, "Mr. President, my advice to you is to take over the Gambia militarily and annex it. The two populations are the same. Behind the French-English divide, everyone speaks the same African languages. If you do take it over, I do not expect that there will be much criticism from the international community. After all, the Gambia has no reason to exist as an independent country. It was a historical mistake."

That startled Senghor, coming from the US ambassador. But he remained true to his devotion to the rule of law. "We can't do that, Mr. Ambassador. It would be a violation of international law. But I tell you what we will do. We will build a road around the Gambia and reroute road traffic that way."

The road was built before I departed Senegal in 1980. I had the feeling that the three-day trip for a truck to circumnavigate the Gambia was just as long as the normal wait to cross the river by ferry. But Senghor felt that Senegal's honor had been upheld.

In his heart of hearts, Senghor saw the Senegalese masses as unready for democracy. He told me once that young Senegalese who could not find employment in the major cities did not have to be unemployed. They could always return to the rural areas and be farmers. Yet, he made no effort to provide agricultural extension, rural infrastructure, irrigation, or basic health services. Senegal was not wealthy, but I had the impression that Senghor and his political friends had assigned their priority to the politically conscious people in the cities. They saw the majority population in the rural countryside as hopelessly mired in their religious and ethnic traditions.

Léopold Senghor was civilized, decent, statesmanlike, and cerebral. At the same time, he remained one of the "strongmen" of Africa. He ruled Senegal for twenty years until his voluntary retirement in 1980, and he did so with an iron fist inside a velvet glove. He did not have to be flamboyant to impress his people. He was generally adored and respected as Senegal's national hero. But he was far from democratic.

In the second decade of the 21st century, a new generation of university-educated Senegalese political leaders is trying to modernize the country and prove Senghor wrong. They have come to power through verified free and fair elections. The initial reports indicate that they are making progress and deserve international support.

The late president Félix Houphouët-Boigny of Côte d'Ivoire greets visiting Assistant Secretary of State Cohen in Abidjan in 1991. Former U.S. ambassador to Abidjan Dennis Kux is on the right.
Credit: USIS Abidjan

CHAPTER 2

Félix Houphouët-Boigny — Côte d'Ivoire

The Farmer President and Destabilizer of Neighbors

Historical Note

Unlike many other African leaders who began their lives in modest circumstances, Félix Houphouët-Boigny was born into a family of African chiefs and wealthy plantation owners in Côte d'Ivoire. When he entered politics in the early 1950s, he was an affluent person who spent a lot of time in Paris involved in the politics of independence from French rule. He sat in the French Parliament as a representative of French West Africa. His first mentors were in the French Communist Party, but he eventually became a conservative in Ivoirien politics. At the time of independence, he was the clear popular choice to be the country's first elected president.

In view of his background as a successful plantation farmer, he favored the peasant farming landowners in his economic policies. By favoring the cocoa planters, he helped create the largest cocoa production in the world. He encouraged the cocoa producers by returning to them a fair share of the world price.

As head of state in francophone Africa's wealthiest country, he exerted significant influence in the neighboring francophone countries, so much so that he initiated profound political changes in his region. His most important initiative was the overthrow by insurgents of Liberia's president Samuel Doe in 1990. He was also a sponsor and mentor of the Angolan rebel leader Jonas Savimbi. In view of France's many private investments in Côte d'Ivoire, Houphouët exercised much influence in French policy toward francophone Africa. After Houphouët's death in 1994, Côte d'Ivoire began a long slow decline into political instability and civil war that lasted until 2012.

I did not have the pleasure of engaging in dialogue with the founding president of Côte d'Ivoire until we were both in the final years of our respective careers. The first time I actually met him was in January 1987 when I accompanied Secretary of State George Shultz on a tour of key African nations. I was representing the National Security Council, where I was senior director for Africa and special assistant to President Reagan. At that time, President Houphouët and I were both seven years away from career end. In 1994, I left the State Department for a new job, and he passed away that same year.

At age 87, Houphouët was a roly-poly little guy whose feet barely reached the floor as he sat facing Shultz and the US delegation. Little in his appearance indicated that he was one of the most powerful heads of state in Africa. Nevertheless, I found Houphouët's discourse at that meeting with Shultz quite refreshing compared to what I had been hearing in other African capitals.

All the other heads of state wanted to discuss grand strategy. Houphouët's preoccupation was with farm prices, as Côte d'Ivoire's wealth was based on tropical farm exports, especially cocoa, coffee, palm oil, and pineapples. His argument that day was that a two-cent increase in the world price for coffee or cocoa would provide more benefits to his country than the total amount of foreign aid. He expressed exasperation at American and European obsession with market prices. He did not understand why the United States could not just decide to fix commodity prices at a level commensurate with fair returns to the producing countries. What were superpowers for, after all?

He came from an extended family of land-owning paramount chiefs centered on south-central Côte d'Ivoire. The family became wealthy exporting pineapples and other tropical fruits and vegetables. He knew from personal experience that agriculture was the core of his country's prosperity, and he never failed to provide maximum support to that sector. Hence, while most African countries had suffered from negative economic growth since independence in 1960, due mainly to over-taxation and discouragement of the farming population, Côte d'Ivoire had become relatively prosperous.

One of France's legacies to its former colonies in Africa was the common currency called the CFA, representing the French African Financial Community. Within the West African segment of that community, a contiguous group of seven nations, Côte d'Ivoire's GDP represented 70 percent of the total.

I started seeing Houphouët regularly between 1988 and 1994 to discuss problems related to the West and Central African regions. It was during these meetings that I learned of his intense interest in dabbling in other countries' affairs. Indeed, he was a master manipulator and destabilizer, but so low key as to be virtually invisible. One of his most important interests was in the former Portuguese colony of Angola in southwest Africa.

The civil war in Angola was of great interest to the United States. It was not just the fact that a Marxist regime was fighting an insurgency representing a "pro-West" rebel group. Above all, it was the presence of 35,000 Cuban troops sent there by President Fidel Castro to keep his friends in power. When Portugal had its internal revolution in 1975, Angola was given immediate independence with virtually no preparation. The anti-Portuguese rebel groups immediately started battling each other for control of power. The Cuban president saw his opportunity to make a splash on the international scene. He sent an expeditionary force to Angola that was instrumental in bringing the MPLA Marxists to power. But the internal war continued, with the "pro-West" insurgents, known as UNITA, controlling a significant area in southeastern Angola. Ironically, one of the important missions of the Cuban force was to guard the oil installations of the American company Chevron against insurgent attacks.

In 1986, President Ronald Reagan announced his doctrine designed to counter Soviet assistance to revolutionary groups anywhere in the world. Because of the Cuban military presence in Angola, Reagan proposed a special covert action program to provide assistance to the UNITA insurgents against the Marxist regime. The program was modest but sufficient to help UNITA protect itself against Soviet-supplied bomber aircraft and armor.

Houphouët entered the Angola picture because he was the mentor of UNITA president Jonas Savimbi, a charismatic personality popular with conservatives in the United States in both political parties. In view of the high priority the White House assigned to support for Savimbi, I considered it important to maintain regular contact with Savimbi. The place I met with him the most often was in the home of President Houphouët-Boigny in Abidjan.

Houphouët liked to guide the discussion. Savimbi and I were discussing the state of US assistance and Savimbi's efforts to achieve recognition from other African countries. Houphouët did not leave us alone to develop our strategies. He was there to preside, putting in his two cents quite often. In short, while the rest of Africa had recognized the MPLA as the legitimate government of Angola, Houphouët, and his colleague Léopold Senghor in Senegal, had decided to support Savimbi. Houphouët's support was clearly the most significant.

While the United States was providing defensive shoulder-fired antiaircraft missiles and antitank weapons to UNITA, Houphouët was providing money-laundering services. Savimbi had a permanent agent in Abidjan who received diamonds from Savimbi's couriers. The diamonds were taken from Angolan fields during UNITA raids and exported as Ivoirien commodities.

My conversations with Houphouët on the Angola issue were in the co-conspiracy mode. It was Houphouët and Cohen trying to remake Angola. He loved it.

During my visits, Houphouët also enjoyed bantering about African matters in general, especially gossip about other heads of state. During one visit in August 1989, I mentioned that I had just been in Addis Ababa, Ethiopia, a week earlier. I told him that I had found Addis rainy, cold, and dull, and President Mengistu a cold fish. I could not imagine any of the hundreds of African diplomats stationed there being happy. His response was, "You can say that again. When we heads of state were debating the headquarters' location of the Organization of African Unity, I was the one who recommended Addis. It was the biggest mistake of my presidency."

In 1989, after the New York agreement of December 1988 had resulted in the departure of Cuban and South African troops from Angola, we turned to the task of encouraging internal peace in Angola. We had no intention of helping UNITA defeat the government of Angola and no possibility of matching the Soviet's massive military assistance to the regime. On the other hand, our assistance to UNITA made it impossible for the regime to defeat the insurgents. Hence, it was a mutually hurting stalemate ripe for resolution.

Our approach was to suggest to Angola's neighbors that they organize a peace process. America's good friend President Mobutu of Zaire, with visions of the Nobel Prize in his head, decided to organize a summit conference in his hometown of Gbadolite, with a large number of African heads of state in attendance. Savimbi was reluctant to attend. He did not want to be intimidated into something he might not want under the pressure of all those heads of state.

I thought the summit a good idea because it was the only game in town. I called Houphouët, who expressed skepticism but agreed that Savimbi should not turn down the request. He agreed to "recommend" that Savimbi show up for the conclave, and Savimbi complied.

The summit meeting ended with a signed "agreement" between Angolan president Dos Santos and Savimbi in which UNITA would win recognition as a political party, and UNITA leaders would enter the government as ministers. The Marxist constitution would remain intact. Savimbi signed the agreement but absolutely did not agree with it. He wanted a "free and fair" election. I wanted to encourage Savimbi to accept—that was about as good as he could expect since he could not win the war. Before I could act, Savimbi's friends in the US conservative community called Secretary of State James Baker, who instructed me to issue a statement saying that anything less than a free and fair election would be unacceptable. I called Houphouët, who confirmed that the agreement was dead on arrival. Houphouët's influence on Savimbi was clearly quite strong, and therefore also his ability to influence US policy. International observers of the Angolan war knew about Soviet support for the regime and American and South African support for UNITA; but

Houphouët's significant role was virtually unknown. He preferred it that way.

While Houphouët's interest in Angola was geostrategic and ideological, more practical was his interest in his northern neighbor, Burkina Faso. Côte d'Ivoire's wealth comes from its position as the world's largest producer of cocoa. Care, feeding, and harvesting of the cocoa tree is heavily labor-intensive. In Côte d'Ivoire, plantation labor is made up mainly of immigrants from Burkina Faso (formerly Upper Volta). Known as "Burkinabe," these immigrant workers and their families make up about 30 percent of the country's population. The plantation workers are not temporary visitors. Most of the families have been in Côte d'Ivoire for generations and thereby constitute a major internal political challenge. Give them full political rights and the entire political balance of the nation would be totally transformed. Above all, the elites of Houphouët's own subregion in the territory of the Baoulé nation could lose their domination of political power.

Houphouët dealt with the problem of immigrant families with finesse. He reasoned that as long as he was alive, he would have no significant opposition. He was supremely popular among both the Ivoirien people and the Burkinabe immigrant population. The only political dissidents who refused to be co-opted into his political family were centered in the University of Côte d'Ivoire, where the faculty constituted a left-wing intellectual opposition to his emphasis on free market capitalism. Houphouët's solution to the immigrant problem was to allow them to vote in presidential elections. Needless to say, he was overwhelmingly reelected every five years. With the right to vote, Houphouët reasoned, the Burkinabe immigrants would feel integrated, even though they really were not, because they were not citizens.

Against the background of Côte d'Ivoire's heavy dependence on immigrant labor, Houphouët needed to keep an eye on his northern neighbor Burkina Faso to make sure that the government there remained friendly and stable. In the early years of the 1980s, Burkina was mainly unstable and less than friendly. During most of the 1970s, a series of military coups had made the government look like a game of musical chairs.

In 1983, Houphouët decided to intervene in his own subtle way. He financed an army coup led by Captains Thomas Sankara and Blaise Compaore. Sankara became the head of state, and Compaore the vice president. Unfortunately for Houphouët, Sankara turned out to be a revolutionary hothead who believed that all of the other heads of state in West Africa were corrupt reactionaries. He traveled all over the region, preaching revolution and scaring some of Houphouët's good friends.

During one of my visits in 1987 to discuss Angola, I chided Houphouët about his selection of Sankara to take over power in Burkina. I accused Sankara of trying to destabilize the entire region of West Africa. Houphouët dismissed my concerns with the flippant remark, "Don't worry, Sankara is just a boy. He will mature quickly." Since we were alone, I insisted that Sankara was hurting the image of the entire French community in West Africa and would eventually hurt Houphouët himself. He took my admonition in without comment; but within a few months, Sankara was violently replaced by Blaise Compaore, who restored political stability to the francophone subregion. Compaore and Houphouët worked so well together that Compaore essentially replaced Houphouët as the dean of French West Africa after Houphouët's death in 1994.

Immediately after my 1987 discussion with Houphouët, I flew up to Ouagadougou, the capital of Burkina Faso, to check things out there. The day of my visit had been declared a holiday because it was the first anniversary of President Reagan's bombing of Libya. Sankara, a great admirer of Gaddafi, had signs hung all over the city denouncing US imperialism. When he talked revolution, therefore, Sankara was using Gaddafi as a role model. Sankara was too busy to see me, but I had a chance to meet Vice President Blaise Compaore for the first time. He received me in army fatigues, a visible pistol in a holster, and with an aggressively negative view of American policy in Africa. I had the feeling that this was not what Houphouët had bargained for. Fortunately, Blaise Compaore turned out to be a reasonable and pragmatic leader after he deposed Sankara. But in selecting him, Houphouët had sown the seeds of Côte d'Ivoire's civil war, which began in 1999, five years after his death, and lasted for twelve agonizing years.

***

Houphouët's last foreign intervention before his death took place in Liberia, right next door. He was a close friend of the late Liberian president William R. Tolbert, whose son had married Houphouët's goddaughter. Much like Houphouët, Tolbert, came from an aristocratic minority, in his case the Americo-Liberians, those descended from the original freed slaves who came to Liberia from the United States, starting in the 1820s. Tolbert was assassinated in a military coup in April 1980.

Not only did Houphouët suffer the shock of his good friend's assassination in cold blood; he had to witness the rise to power of a bunch of illiterate Liberian army enlisted men led by one Sergeant Samuel Doe. The crowning blow came from the violation of the French ambassador's residence in Monrovia, where Tolbert's son had taken refuge. Some of Doe's officers forced their way into the ambassador's house, took Tolbert's son prisoner, and summarily executed him. Houphouët never forgot that. He took his revenge ten years later.

On Christmas Eve 1989, a group of about two hundred guerrilla fighters crossed the border from Côte d'Ivoire into Liberia and began an insurgency designed to overthrow President Doe. The insurgency was promoted and financed by Houphouët, supported logistically by Burkina president Compaore, and supplied by Libyan "leader" Muammar Gaddafi. The guerrillas marched toward the capital city of Monrovia, picking up additional fighters along the way, as President Doe's army responded with the burning of villages and the perpetration of massive human rights atrocities.

The guerrillas were under the command of Charles Taylor, a former high official in Doe's regime who had been trained in guerrilla tactics in Libya. Taylor's forces were able to arrive at the gates of Monrovia in about six weeks. Much to Houphouët's chagrin, some of the leaders of the Economic Community of West African States (ECOWAS), of which Côte d'Ivoire was a member, wanted to intervene to stop a Taylor takeover. In an ECOWAS summit meeting designed to reach consensus on what, if anything, to do about Liberia, Côte d'Ivoire and Burkina Faso passionately argued against any intervention. Their man Charles Taylor was doing very well, thank you.

Burkina and Côte d'Ivoire's joint veto should normally have prevented an ECOWAS intervention, because decisions to take such actions had to be unanimous. But Nigeria, Sierra Leone, Guinea, and Ghana decided to move ahead without consensus and sent a military force to Liberia to block Taylor from taking over. The force was called ECOMOG and had as its mission to establish peace and a democratic transition. But Charles Taylor refused to accept West African peacekeeping and brought ECOMOG under heavy artillery fire. This was the beginning of Liberia's destructive seven-year civil war between Taylor and ECOMOG.

In the State Department, our instructions were to refrain from diplomatic intervention. We were told not to "take charge" of the Liberian problem. In August 1990, I was instructed to do a tour of the countries involved in the war, with a stop at the US Embassy in Monrovia, to demonstrate that we were not totally disinterested. While we decided to be inactive, we needed to demonstrate sympathetic interest in Liberia's troubles. That country, after all, was our most reliable friend in Africa.

Needless to say, an important stop on my itinerary was Abidjan for a conversation with Houphouët. I asked him what he could tell me about Taylor's insurgency. As Taylor's supplies and reinforcements were transiting Côte d'Ivoire, Houphouët's position was crucial.

Houphouët's response reinforced his image as the *eminence grise* who did his dirty work from deep behind the scenes. He knew that I knew about his heavy support for Taylor. Ivoirien security forces were transporting Libyan arms from Ouagadougou to Taylor's lines through Côte d'Ivoire. Yet, his poker face was unchanging. He said, "I have never met Charles Taylor. I do not know Charles Taylor. I have nothing to do with Charles Taylor."

Ignoring his lies, I pleaded with Houphouët to use his position as the region's senior statesman to try to bring about peace between Taylor and ECOMOG so that Liberia could move ahead with a democratic political process. Houphouët had received a request from the United States that he could not refuse. He thus proceeded to call a summit conference of all protagonists. The conference took place and achieved nothing, but Houphouët had covered his tracks.

Two years later, during an international conference in Abidjan, I asked Burkina president Blaise Compaore why he and Houphouët had decided to sponsor Taylor's insurgency. The war was in its second year at that moment, and Liberia was in a state of total collapse. Liberia had become a humanitarian disaster. Compaore said, in all sincerity, that he and Houphouët considered Samuel Doe a disgrace to Liberia and to the entire region. I agreed with his assessment. He then acknowledged, however, that Taylor was a bad choice, and that he was destroying Liberia.

I responded with a question. "Will you now stop supplying Taylor with arms in order to pressure him into peace talks with ECOMOG?"

Compaore said "yes."

Unfortunately, his assistance to Taylor continued for five more years. His and Houphouët's investment in Taylor was too large to stop at that point. They had to see it through to victory.

During his long tenure as Côte d'Ivoire's president, Houphouët loved to keep his top political cronies in a state of apprehension about their own careers. During my time as assistant secretary, I witnessed a number of incidents that demonstrated this. I remember being called by a French friend who was a high-level lobbyist and bag carrier for a number of African heads of state. He asked if I would be willing to have a private dinner in Washington with a high-level Ivoirien official who wanted it kept absolutely secret. He said he could not give me the name because he feared it might leak but asked me to trust him. The person would be very high level. I accepted the request. The visitor turned out to be Henri Konan Bédié, president of the National Assembly and first in line to succeed to the presidency if Houphouët died. Here was this very powerful politician living in fear of upstaging Houphouët himself. Having dinner with the US assistant secretary of state was totally reserved for the president himself.

Among the many sectors that Houphouët reserved for himself was control over francophone Africa's money. During the colonial period, the French administration had established a common currency for its African colonies, the CFA Franc, meaning "common francophone African" franc. Tied to the French franc and totally guaranteed by the French Treasury, the CFA was considered a hard currency.

Toward 1989 and through the early part of the 1990s, at a rate of 50 CFA to one French franc, it was clear that the CFA was much overvalued. This was hurting the economies of the twelve African countries involved. Imports were too cheap, thereby encouraging excessive unneeded imports by urban populations. Exports, especially agricultural products, were not earning sufficient local currency to give the farmers a decent living. Government budgets were strained because of the low flow of local currency revenue.

Around 1991, economists, especially those at the World Bank, were starting to call for a devaluation of the CFA franc to a more realistic level. Unfortunately, both Houphouët and the French Treasury considered that a bad idea. Houphouët wanted the urban elites to continue to be able to purchase imported products from Europe. The French government at the time had managed to stabilize the value of the French franc and did not want to do anything that might undermine it. My own feeling then was that the French really had no objection to devaluing, but were afraid to go against Houphouët.

During 1991, when I was traveling through Paris on my way home from one of my frequent trips to Africa, the press section of the American embassy in Paris asked if I would preside over a luncheon debate with journalists specializing in African issues. The group was rather sizable, representing both French and African media. The format called for me to give a short summary of US policy in Africa and then take questions from the journalists, on the record.

Toward the end, a French journalist asked how the United States government regarded the ongoing debate about the exchange rate of the CFA franc. Showing strong feelings, I said that African economies were hurting badly because of the serious overvaluation of the CFA. I called for a major devaluation. I was speaking not just for State's Bureau of African Affairs, but for the US Treasury Department and Secretary of State James Baker, who had spoken about the CFA on several occasions.

It must have been a slow news day because the newspapers gave my statement significant coverage. When I arrived in Washington the next day, I saw a message from the French minister of finance to the US secretary of the Treasury denouncing my on-the-record statement to the French and African press. He called my statement an unacceptable interference in France's internal affairs and my analysis of the economic situation in francophone Africa not accurate. On the other hand, I received phone calls from Secretary Baker's office and my friends in the Treasury's Office of African Nations congratulating me. A week later, the French minister of overseas cooperation came to Washington to meet with the World Bank and USAID. The French ambassador asked me to meet the minister for breakfast. The minister continued to admonish me for my statement to the point where I promised not to say anything more on the subject in public.

Houphouët said nothing to me about the CFA issue, but I was sure he was behind the French reaction. A devaluation of the CFA would have been a big blow to his ego. After his 1994 death, I was working at the Global Coalition for Africa, housed in the World Bank. One afternoon, as I was walking in the hall, the World Bank vice president for Africa, Kim Jaycox, saw me and called me into his office suite. Champagne corks were popping. What was the occasion? The French treasury had just announced the devaluation of the CFA from 50 CFA for one French Franc to 100 to one. Shortly thereafter, when I visited Houphouët's successor in Abidjan, Henri Konan Bédié, I asked him how much of the additional local currency generated by the devaluation would be going to the farmers. He said, "Two hundred percent." In other words, he claimed that the double amount of local currency would all go to the farmers. I did not believe it, because a sizable percentage of farm export earnings were secretly diverted to finance the ruling political party. But I was sure that the farmers would be doing better in any event.

How did Houphouët set the stage for Côte d'Ivoire's civil war that ensued after his death?

In 1991, I had a visit in Washington from a high Ivoirien official in town for talks with the World Bank. He asked to see me to deliver a message from Houphouët. He said that Houphouët was planning to run for reelection in 1992. However, he would announce his retirement in 1993 after serving only one year. In addition, Houphouët had designated my visitor to be his successor. I expressed satisfaction, because my visitor was considered one of the most capable of the Ivoirien officials.

As it happened, Houphouët did run for reelection in 1992. He won, of course, but did not announce his retirement in 1993 as my earlier visitor had predicted. He just carried on. In those final months prior to his death, when his health was clearly failing and he was absent for long periods, I saw him several times in Paris. During one visit, he told me that he was staying away from Abidjan for lengthy periods in order to test the younger leaders and determine if they were up to the job.

When Houphouët died in 1994, the person who thought he had been designated as the successor found himself in the wrong position. The constitution designated the president of the National Assembly to be the successor to serve until the next election. The constitutional successor was sworn in, but the disappointed aspirant began a process, supported by President Compaore of Burkina Faso, to destabilize the political system, leading to a twelve-year civil conflict and a greatly weakened Côte d'Ivoire.

When I told some of my Ivoirien friends the story of the official who had told me that Houphouët had sincerely promised that he would be his successor, they informed me that Houphouët undoubtedly made the same promise to at least ten politicians working in his government.

One of Houphouët's enduring legacies for Côte d'Ivoire was the Roman Catholic Basilica Our Lady of Peace, which he had built in his home town of Yamoussoukro, about eighty miles north of Abidjan. Modeled on St. Peter's in Rome, the basilica was completed in 1989 at a cost of $300 million. Houphouët insisted that all of the money came from his family's personal fortunes, but nobody believed him. I visited the building in early 1990, and I found it an architectural masterpiece. All of the giant doors remain open during masses so that the congregation can see they are in Africa at all times, regardless of where they are seated. At the same time, the air- conditioning remains powerful, even with the doors open.

During a visit to the Vatican's Foreign Ministry in Rome shortly after my visit to the Basilica Our Lady of Peace, I was invited out on the ministry's balcony overlooking St. Peter's. I remarked to my host that the view strongly resembled the basilica in Yamoussoukro. My host frowned and said, "We consider the basilica to be a tremendous extravagance for a poor African country. To make matters worse, Houphouët wants to give it to the Pope. We are try-ing to dodge this one, but we will not be able to do so." The pope consecrated the Basilica in September 1990.

When it comes to African monuments to satisfy big egos, Houphouët's basilica was the absolute winner. Unfortunately, he could not accept the idea that he might personally see his successor sworn in while he was still alive. He had to die with his boots on. In this context, Senegal president Léopold Senghor was the franco-phone African head of state with the greatest prestige as he bowed out voluntarily at age eighty in 1980.

The late president of the Republic of Gabon, Omar Bongo Ondimba in 1995.
Credit: ZIOPICS.com

CHAPTER 3

Albert-Bernard Bongo
(El Hadj Omar Bongo Ondimba)
—Gabon

Historical Note

If any of the early African heads of state had a sweetheart deal, it was Albert-Bernard Bongo of the Republic of Gabon, who served as president from 1967 to 2009. El Hadj Omar Bongo came to power almost by accident and remained head of state for forty-four years, almost through pure inertia. Gabon's first president after independence was Léon Mba, the leader of Gabon's anti-colonial movement. Mba came from the Fang ethnic community, the largest single ethnic grouping in the country. Bongo was Mba's vice president. He was from the Teke ethnic group and had been selected for ethnic balance.

The former French colony, perched right on the equator on the Atlantic coast in central Africa, has been underpopulated and rich in resources to this very day. Bongo was vice president when the founding president, Leon Mba, died a natural death in 1967. Bongo settled in as the new president, knowing that he had full security under the protection of a French military garrison. Unlike other former colonies in Africa, there was no way the government of Gabon could be overthrown in a military coup. In addition, Bongo hired a well-trained personal security contingent from Morocco to make sure he was safe both in his palace and during his public appearances.

Thus freed of any fear of being overthrown or assassinated, Bongo could relax and devote his time to personal and family enrichment. Significant deposits of crude oil had been discovered offshore at about the time Bongo came to power. A steady stream of revenue from oil royalties gave him financial security. What could be a better deal than that?

To his credit, Bongo did not spend all of his time amassing wealth. He also cared about stability in the central African region. He was quite ready to supply his good offices to settle disputes. Bongo is one of the few African heads of state who succeeded in founding a dynasty. After his death in 2009, his son Ali Ben Bongo was elected president. Ali had been minister of defense for two decades before succeeding his father.

My first official diplomatic encounter with Bongo took place in 1971, when the US government was called upon to assist an American company that was being threatened with confiscation in neighboring Central African Republic (CAR). My title at that point in my career was Director for Central African Affairs.

The president of the CAR was a mentally unstable former French Army sergeant named Jean-Bedel Bokassa, who had served in Vietnam and subsequently took power in a military coup. The American company was the principal buyer of raw artisanal diamonds, the country's main source of revenue. Bokassa assumed that if he confiscated the American company, all the diamond revenue would revert to his control. He did not have a clue about the sanctity of contracts or the protection of foreign investments.

When I approached Bongo with a request that he persuade Bokassa to be reasonable and act pursuant to international law, Bongo agreed immediately. However, he said he needed some "persuasion money." He could not go and visit his neighboring head of state empty-handed and thought that fifty thousand dollars would be sufficient. In 1971, that amount was still considered attractive. The funds were identified through private sources and, true to his word, Bongo persuaded Bokassa to negotiate within the confines of the agreement with the company. From that point on, Bongo and I became buddies.

I was under no illusions. Of all the former French colonies in Africa, Gabon under Bongo remained the most loyal to Paris. He had a direct line to the French presidency, and he never refused a request from his French mentors.

Much later, toward the end of Bongo's reign, the French

government had a diminishing interest in the special relationship with its former colonies, known as France-Afrique. Investigative reporting in the Parisian press during the early years of the twenty-first century revealed that Bongo was an equal opportunity financial supporter of both the French Gaullist and Socialist parties. Against this background, I knew that the United States could never hope for a special relationship with Gabon; but Bongo enjoyed teasing his French mentors through his friendly ties to American diplomats throughout the decades of his power. We took full advantage of that.

Bongo was a short man, about five feet one inch. This apparently bothered him. To compensate, he wore high heels. He also had an insatiable need to seduce an endless supply of new women. During his travels, he was usually accompanied by at least one attractive young female, whom he introduced as his "personal secretary." There was a new one every trip.

In the mid-1980s, Bongo needed a change in the Gabonese marriage law to better accommodate his serial seductions. When a couple marries in Gabon, they are required to choose whether the marriage will be monogamous or polygamous. That initial decision cannot be changed. Bongo married his first wife under the monogamy regime, before he became president. In the mid-1980s, he decided that monogamy was interfering with his sexual appetites. He decided to introduce legislation authorizing the male partner to change from monogamy to polygamy after the beginning of the marriage. That proposal unleashed a series of female demonstrations in the streets of Gabon's capital, Libreville. Bongo was forced to back down.

His failure to change the law did not stop him from his lubricious ways. After I left the US government in 1994, I visited Libreville on a commercial business assignment. For the first time since I had known him, he invited me to the family quarters for lunch. There were at least fifteen small children there, attended by as many nannies. His need to seduce was matched by his ability to procreate.

Also in the mid-1980s, Bongo was invited to Libya for an official visit to Muammar Gaddafi, the North African oil-rich country's all-powerful "Leader." While there, Bongo decided that he should convert from Catholicism to Islam. He took the name Omar Bongo Ondimba. At the time, we all assumed that a monetary incentive was involved, since Gaddafi liked to spread money around to buy African friendships. But we saw nothing on the surface immediately.

In 1991, I received a call from an old banking acquaintance working in Citibank's private banking office in Paris. My friend informed me that President Bongo had deposited into his Citibank account in Libreville a check for one million US dollars, issued by the central bank of Libya. Since Libya was at that time subject to US financial sanctions, all American banks were under US government orders to confiscate and freeze all Libyan financial instruments. Needless to say, Bongo was not happy. He demanded that Citibank return his check. He was threatening to eject the bank from Gabon.

Upon receiving this news, I called the Office of Foreign Assets Control (OFAC) in the US Department of the Treasury. The confiscation of the Libyan check was confirmed. I asked if there was a provision in the sanctions regulations allowing for a waiver based on US national interest criteria. I was informed that a waiver on foreign policy grounds was possible if I requested it. However, the Treasury Department was required by law to publish the waiver in the Federal Register, thereby letting the world know that Bongo was taking Libyan money. I told OFAC to issue the waiver. I knew that Bongo would not be upset to see his name in print, even in that context.

Bongo was very conscious of Gabon's reputation as a total fiefdom of France. He was therefore looking for every opportunity to show his independence. Part of his strategy was to seek attention from American presidents. Needless to say, American presidents were not that interested in him.

During the period January 1987 to January 1989, I was assigned to the National Security Council as special assistant to President Ronald Reagan and director for African affairs. My main work during that time was to support Assistant Secretary of State for African Affairs Chester Crocker in his successful effort to bring about the independence of Namibia in southwest Africa. Among my unwanted distractions were steady visits and phone calls from mutual friends asking that President Bongo be invited to the White House on an official visit. Needless to say, Bongo was not on anyone's priority list.

But Bongo got lucky in 1988. One routine day, I was attending the national security advisor's daily staff meeting that began at 7:30 a.m. in the White House situation room. My colleague covering Middle Eastern affairs reported that the king of Morocco had canceled his official visit to the White House a mere three weeks before the event was scheduled. It was embarrassing, and Mrs. Reagan was upset because so many plans had been set in motion.

Remembering the many pleas I had been receiving on behalf of Bongo, I meekly chimed in: "I know a head of state willing to come to Washington on short notice." My mention of Bongo did not cause heartburn because he was, after all, very "pro-West" in his foreign policy and highly friendly to the private sector. So, Bongo was invited on short notice. He accepted without hesitation.

President Reagan was a gracious and friendly host. He quickly put Bongo at ease, and they had a relaxed discussion. The problem was that there were not that many subjects of mutual interest. American investors were being well treated in Gabon. The flow of Gabonese manganese and uranium was steady and reliable. Gabon was a reliable ally in the United Nations. Substantive issues kept up the discussion during the first hour in the White House cabinet room, but during the subsequent luncheon, all the dossiers had been exhausted.

Bongo broke the ice at lunch by launching a "complaint." "You know, Mr. President, your Peace Corps volunteers are causing me embarrassment."

Reagan took on a serious demeanor: "Tell me about it."

"Well, it's like this. I go back to my home village in southeastern Gabon about once a month. There is this Peace Corps volunteer living and working there, right in the village."

Reagan jumped in and said, "That is what he is supposed to be doing, helping the rural farmers improve their lives. What's wrong with that?"

With tongue slightly in cheek, Bongo said, "But he speaks our tribal language better than me. He is making me look stupid."

Bongo's remark truly relaxed all of us, and from that point on, Reagan kept telling jokes, right through dessert and coffee. What was fascinating about the joke telling was the delayed laughter. Bongo could not understand a word of English. After Reagan finished a joke, the Americans laughed right away. After the translation, the Gabonese visitors had their delayed laughs.

Knowing that I was the one responsible for the official White House invitation, Bongo became even more of a buddy than before.

In early 1989, I went from the National Security Council job to the State Department, where President George H. W. Bush appointed me Assistant Secretary of State for Africa. In that capacity I had two occasions to call upon Bongo's friendship.

In 1989, the Gabonese government decided to hold an auction for fifteen offshore oil exploration blocks. Several American oil companies decided to submit bids. Until that point, the French oil company Elf Aquitaine had a monopoly on oil production in Gabon. We were all surprised that Bongo suddenly felt courageous enough to look beyond the French.

The day of the scheduled opening of bids, the oil company representatives gathered in Libreville were informed that the auction was cancelled and all of the blocks had been awarded to Elf Aquitaine. The American companies that had spent a lot of time and money to prepare their bids were furious. A few called me to complain. I decided to call Bongo directly and convey Washington's displeasure.

Bongo was clearly embarrassed by what happened. His explanation was not unexpected. "You know, Mr. Minister, that we have special ties to France. Paris insists that our oil be kept in the francophone family. I could not refuse."

I responded that we were quite disappointed. "After all, Mr. President, you were the guest of President Reagan in the White House quite recently. All we ask is fair treatment."

After a long pause, Bongo suddenly perked up. "I have an idea Mr. Minister. Under the production sharing agreement we signed with Elf for these fifteen blocks, the Gabonese government has a 45 percent carried ownership interest. There is nothing to stop us from selling all or part of that 45 percent to outside companies." Thus, some American companies were able to get a foot in the door to Gabonese oil production.

On a higher diplomatic level, I decided to encourage Bongo

to become involved in the Angolan peace process. The December 1988 New York agreement brokered by Assistant Secretary of State Chester Crocker provided for a transition to independence of the Southwest Africa territory controlled by South Africa. This was the future Republic of Namibia. Also included in the New York agreement was the departure of both Cuban and South African troops from Angola.

With the change of administrations from Reagan to Bush in 1989, there remained unfinished business in Angola. The Marxist government of Angola was locked in an insurgent war against a "pro-West" guerilla movement known as UNITA. In 1986, President Reagan had decided to provide defensive weapons to UNITA in response to the Soviet Union's massive military assistance to the Angolan government. When President Bush came into office in 1989, there was no longer any reason for outside interests to be involved in Angola's civil conflict. The Cold War was ending, Cuban troops had departed Angola, and the Soviets under Gorbachev were no longer interested in supporting so-called "Marxist brothers" in Africa.

Since the United States was supporting one of the sides in the Angolan war, we could not initiate a peace process. In view of his previous successes in the central African regions, I asked Bongo to try to persuade the Angolan president, Eduardo dos Santos, to come to the negotiating table with UNITA. Bongo agreed and called a conference of regional heads of state in order to persuade President Dos Santos to look to negotiations rather than continued war against UNITA. Dos Santos agreed, thus beginning a long and arduous peace process that continued under President Mobutu of Zaire and ended in a peace agreement in 1991.

France's strong ties to its former African colonies have been quite strong since the independence wave during the 1960s. Over time, and with a change of generations, most of the ties became less paternalistic and more those of relationships of equals. Gabon under Bongo was the exception. France remained in an almost consular relationship with Gabon well into the twenty-first century. The number of French expatriates in Gabon has remained higher than the average in sub-Saharan Africa.

During one of my visits in 1991, I arrived in Libreville on a Sunday. Two of the embassy staff invited me to have lunch at one of the many restaurants on the beach. Most of the diners were expatriates. At a nearby table, I could not help but overhear some of the conversation. One of the French ladies at the table said that she had just arrived in Libreville after a month's vacation in France. "It's so great to be back home here in Libreville," the lady said. "France is just impossible." Those days are gone forever in most African countries, but not in Gabon.

During my four years in office as assistant secretary of state, the United States and Gabon achieved together something important beyond Bongo's helpful efforts at regional conflict resolution. Using appropriated funds, we started in Gabon a project called the Congo Basin Initiative, to conserve the equatorial forest of central Africa. President Bongo was fully cooperative, and other governments in the region followed his example. This was especially true of the Republic of Congo under President Denis Sassou Ngueso. In both countries, there are now thousands of square miles of forest in which both logging and hunting are prohibited, with funds allocated to enforcement. In one major uninhabited forest that straddles the border between Gabon and the Congo, American scientists found in 2011 a population of approximately ten thousand chimpanzees.

Bongo had a sweetheart deal as one of Africa's luckiest heads of state. Gabon has about 250,000 square kilometers of land, about the size of the American state of Colorado. With a small population of only 1.6 million people, Gabon could easily have become a wealthy country during Bongo's forty-four years in power. Oil production of 250,000 barrels a day, combined with significant earnings from uranium, iron ore, manganese, and lumber, could have financed a modern education system, advanced infrastructure, and highly productive tropical agriculture. But after forty-four years, Gabon had little to show for all that natural wealth. Instead, Bongo left significant private property in Paris's wealthiest residential areas, as well as cash in a number of private banks. Above all, he left a nation of overwhelmingly poor people.

Bongo's replacement as head of state is his son Ali Ben Bongo, a university-educated, experienced government official. Let us hope that he can break the reactionary hold over Gabon of a few families, including his own, and make up for a half century of lost time.

GROUP II

The British Commonwealth:
Missed Opportunities for Greatness

Daniel Arap Moi, former president of the Republic of Kenya, addressing an election rally in Nairobi, November 1992.
Credit: ITS254.com

CHAPTER 4

Daniel Arap Moi—Kenya

"Now it is our turn to eat"

Historical Note

Like Omar Bongo of Gabon, Daniel Arap Moi of Kenya was an accidental president. The first Kenyan president and founding father was Jomo Kenyatta, one of the great heroes of the anticolonial struggle against the British. In the run-up to independence in 1963, Kenya had two nationalist political parties, Kenyatta's Kenyan African National Union (KANU), and Arap Moi's Kenyan African Democratic Union (KADU). There was no possibility that KADU could win the election against Kenyatta the national hero. Arap Moi, therefore, did not hesitate to accept Kenyatta's invitation to merge the two parties as well as his proposal that Moi join the ticket as vice president.

Kenyatta was president of Kenya from 1963 until his death in 1978. As vice president, Moi acceded to the presidency automatically, pursuant to the constitution. As president, he was able to seize control of KANU, thereby assuring his regular re-election every five years. In addition, Kenya followed the example of the majority of other newly independent African countries by establishing a constitutional one-party state. Opposition political parties were not allowed to exist. Competition for power, therefore, had to take place within the single party. As president, Moi did not have to stand for election in primary contests. But the party did allow the voters to have a free choice in their selection of members of Parliament, thereby assuring a certain amount of political turnover.

Moi was president from 1978 until 2002 when he retired voluntarily. His administration was marked by some major corruption scandals and by some mysterious deaths of political personalities. Like most of the important political personalities, Moi favored his own ethnic group, the Kalenjin, in his appointments and patronage. Overall, his administration exercised tight controls over all economic activity, thereby discouraging private investment by both internal and external investors. Moi tried very hard to fight the trend toward multiparty democracy that was growing in Africa, but was forced to change the constitution in 1991.

Upon his retirement in 2002, Moi tried to influence the choice of his successor, but failed. During the colonial period, Moi had been an educator and a prominent leader of the evangelical church. Although he changed the constitution to allow for multiparty politics and multiparty elections, he made no effort to defuse the high tensions of ethnic rivalries and hatred that continue to pervade Kenyan politics as of early 2015.

I did not start doing diplomatic business with Moi until 1989 when he had already been president for eleven years. Our relations with Kenya were consistently excellent. Moi and his ministers were generally sympathetic to American interests and objectives in East Africa. The United States and Kenya were usually on the same wavelength with respect to the major international issues of the day. We had an excellent support program for Kenya's air force, one of the few in Africa. My consultations with Moi and his top ministers were mostly about regional issues, such as the civil wars in Sudan and Mozambique.

During my visits to Moi in State House, I found him friendly but one of the stiffest heads of state in Africa. Every move was ceremonial. Despite the one-party state, Kenya had a lively and relatively free media. The political atmosphere was relaxed. There were few, if any, political prisoners.

During the second half of 1989, Kenya's internal political situation started to become confrontational. The constitutional one-party state came under fire from intellectuals. The demand for political reform started out as an issue for intellectuals, but gradually gained steam as the middle class and business community took up the cause in public. In addition to the natural desire for more political choice, there was a certain fatigue with the corruption and excessive economic controls. Moi's dour personality did not help him deflect the growing pro-democracy movement.

Into this volatile mix of growing political discontent walked a new American ambassador, Mr. Smith Hempstone. A career journalist and one of his generation's most knowledgeable experts on sub-Saharan Africa, Hempstone unwittingly became the catalyst that transformed Kenyan politics.

During his preparations in Washington prior to arriving in Nairobi to take up his ambassadorial assignment, Hempstone participated in a weeklong meeting of all American ambassadors serving in Africa. It was the month of June 1989. During the discussions, he was on a panel discussing the promotion of democracy in Africa. Earlier, we heard from Secretary of State James Baker that President George H. W. Bush had decided to step up democracy promotion worldwide. Hempstone's panel was discussing the impact of this new policy on our diplomacy in Africa where the one-party state was still very much entrenched.

Hempstone argued that in a friendly country like Kenya, where political stability was strong, we should not be rocking the boat about democracy. Sure, let's support the growth of democracy, but in Kenya, let's not pound the table. Some Kenyan intellectuals are going around preaching about the need for multiparty democracy, but there is no need for the United States to get directly involved.

Shortly thereafter, Hempstone arrived in Nairobi and jumped into the full panoply of diplomatic activity. He and his dynamic spouse were full participants in the cut and thrust of political debate. One of his early activities was a luncheon speech at the very prestigious Nairobi Rotary Club. The main point of his speech was to alert the Kenyan elite about the growing importance of democracy promotion in American foreign policy. He went so far as to predict that governments that did not demonstrate the political willingness to begin a visible transition to democracy could suffer a decline of US largesse. He did not offer the caveat that Kenya need not worry in view of its stability and importance to US interests in the Horn of Africa.

With the media present, Hempstone's remarks created a bombshell. The headlines in Kenya's widely circulating press told Kenyans that the United States would be exerting heavy pressure on the Kenyan government to accept multiparty democracy. This provided a breath of fresh air to the pro-democracy intellectuals. They felt empowered by the president of the United States. They became even more vocal in denouncing the one-party state, and started to attack President Moi himself for being on the wrong side of history.

Hempstone himself became a popular hero. He was "Mr. Democracy" in Kenya. He was constantly in demand as a speaker before organizations. In a change of outlook from the time he debated the issue in Washington, Hempstone became a strong advocate for an opening to democracy in Kenya. He crossed the red line that says American diplomats should refrain from interfering in the host country's internal affairs.

President Moi did not take kindly to the newly empowered intellectuals who had become shrill in demanding democracy. Neither did he take kindly to Ambassador Hempstone's pro-democracy advocacy. His first action was to place some of the leading Kenyan pro-democracy advocates under "preventive detention" using laws enacted by the UK colonialists during their war against Mau Mau guerrilla fighters who were attacking isolated British farmers during the 1950s.

The pro-democracy advocates were placed under detention because of their subversive activity against the Kenyan constitution. Needless to say, the jailing of persons merely because they are advocating for democracy caught the attention of human rights groups in Europe and the United States.

In the late summer of 1989, I received a call from Senator Nancy Kassebaum of Kansas, the chairperson of the Senate Foreign Relations Subcommittee on Africa. She told me that President Moi's actions against pro-democracy advocates were becoming politically troublesome. She warned me that our very important military cooperation program with the Kenyan Air Force could be in jeopardy. The Congress did not want to be supplying military hardware to human rights violators.

Having received Senator Kassebaum's message loud and clear, I decided to travel to Nairobi to talk to President Moi. He agreed to receive me shortly after my arrival. Hempstone and I went to the presidential palace together. There, we received the first shot across our bow. Ambassador Hempstone was kindly requested to wait in the outer lounge while I was admitted for a private conversation with President Moi. Needless to say, Hempstone was devastated, but he kept a stiff upper lip. After all, he had become the popular hero of the Nairobi press.

That first meeting with Moi was friendly but very stiff. He had an absolute need to appear presidential. I explained that his good friends in Washington, including influential members of the United States Congress, were becoming nervous about the detention of prominent Kenyan intellectuals merely because they were making public declarations calling for multiparty democracy. They were responding to growing pressure from human rights groups. There was no African nation that was better known in the United States than Kenya.

Moi reflected on my statement for a while and then said forcefully, "OK, I will release all of them. They are not worth the food that we feed them." However, he did not say that he would move to change the constitution to allow for multiparty democracy.

The conversation then turned to the civil war in Mozambique, a subject of particular interest to Moi. I told him that President Bush has persuaded Mozambican president Joaquim Chissano to accept negotiations with the rebel group RENAMO. Chissano and his political associates had been demanding that the international community deal with RENAMO because these rebels were being supported by the white minority regime in South Africa. Bush told Chissano that he could not expect the international community to intervene and that negotiations between Mozambicans were the only option.

Moi said that he agreed with President Bush's approach, and asked about the next steps. I told him that the leader of RENAMO, Alphonse Dhlakama, was a clandestine leader who did not communicate easily. He was highly suspicious of the good relations between the Western government and the Mozambican government. He considered Chissano to be a Marxist authoritarian who confiscated church properties, murdered traditional chiefs, and had no intention of allowing any form of democracy. I also told him that RENAMO's reputation in the West was very negative. The organization's human rights violations were considered to be the most violent and heinous. Support for negotiations would not be easy.

Moi said that he knew Dhlakama very well. They were both active evangelical Christians. "How can people accuse Dhlakama of being a human rights violator when he goes around giving out Bibles?" Moi declared rather vehemently. I knew then that Moi would be our channel to Dhlakama. I asked him if he could help us reach out to the RENAMO leader. He agreed instantly, and assigned his foreign minister Bethwel Kipalagat to be our liaison.

After that first meeting, I thought that US-Kenyan relations were back on a friendly track. Moi had promised to release the political detainees, and would be helpful in our efforts to get negotiations going in the Mozambique civil war. Ambassador Hempstone disagreed. He said that he did not expect Moi to release the detainees. He was too stubborn and paranoid when it came to internal politics.

Hempstone was right. Moi did not release the political detainees. Following the British colonial law to the letter, Moi was required to review each detainee's situation monthly. So, he had the personal task of renewing each detention. He could not escape the issue by delegating to someone else. One evening in late 1989 Hempstone called me at home. He said that one of the Kenyan democracy advocates had knocked on his residence door and requested asylum from Moi's repression. He was expecting to be arrested and placed under preventive detention. Hempstone asked for my instructions. I said, "Smith, send him away. We cannot have another long-term resident in an American ambassador's residence." Hempstone's response was, "OK, but you will be responsible if he dies in custody."

Toward the end of 1989 and the beginning of 1990, the political detention situation had become so bad that the US Congress decided to suspend our military assistance program. I saw Moi again in March 1990 in Windhoek, Namibia, at the ceremonies marking Namibia's independence from South Africa. I told him that I had warned him about the detentions causing problems with the US Congress. He waived that issue away, and insisted on talking about Mozambique and the peace process. It was clear that he needed foreign affairs to keep him from thinking too much about domestic issues.

The detention problem, as well as the growing repression of dissidents by the police and intelligence services, continued throughout 1990 and into 1991. The nation that had been something of a poster child for an African open society was sinking into the main stream of corrupt African authoritarianism.

In mid-1991, the international community, under State Department leadership, decided to put collective pressure on the Moi regime. In July 1991, all of the international economic development donors, including the apolitical World Bank and IMF, decided to suspend all aid to Kenya. I was personally amazed at how fast we could achieve unanimous action. When I announced the project at the secretary of state's morning staff meeting, Deputy Secretary Larry Eagleburger asked me when the coordinated action was scheduled to begin. I said that it would begin one week later. Eagleburger responded that such an action was so unprecedented and significant that I should have given the secretary's office more advanced notice. This action gave Moi the opportunity to persuade the political hardliners in the KANU party to accept the idea of amending the constitution to abolish the one party state and establish multiparty democracy.

The first multiparty election was held in December 1992. Because of Moi's general unpopularity, we expected him to be defeated. But he surprised us by winning with only 38 percent of the vote. The Kenyan system does not call for a runoff between the two highest candidates. A simple plurality is sufficient.

The establishment of multiparty democracy in Kenya resulted in the lifting of all suspensions of foreign assistance, and relations returned to normal. As far as the Mozambique war was concerned, the quiet assistance provided by Moi and Kipalagat was essential. They arranged for me to have several secret meetings with RENAMO in Malawi, the country that South Africa was using as a transit base for shipping arms and supplies to RENAMO. At those meetings, I was able to persuade Dhlakama that we would work for win-win negotiations leading to a free vote in Mozambique. As a result, the negotiations mediated by the Italian Catholic lay organization in Rome, Sant'Egidio, with considerable assistance from the State Department, was able to reach a peace agreement that led to an end to the civil war in Mozambique.

In general, Moi was one our best friends in Africa. He never refused any of our requests, including rights to use the port of Mombasa and the international airport at Nairobi for US military movements in the Indian Ocean. For a while, we even had a US naval base in Mombasa as well as an American consulate there. On the economic side, Nairobi was the favorite place in East Africa for American business operations. When American forces were sent to Somalia in November 1992, our use of the Nairobi airport was totally open.

As in a number of other countries in Africa until the end of 1990s, we had the dilemma in Kenya of Moi's great cooperation in bilateral relations as opposed to his corrupt governance, with occasional sinister overtones. During the second half of 1990, Moi was in Washington for a World Bank meeting. We did not recommend that President Bush receive him, because he was still engaged in detaining democracy advocates. He invited me to breakfast at his hotel where the conversation was about US activities in Africa. We did not talk about Kenyan politics, because he had heard from me too many times on that subject.

Conspicuous by his absence from that breakfast was Foreign Minister Robert Ouko. We knew he was in Washington and he would normally be expected to accompany President Moi during his diplomatic discussions in foreign countries. On the other hand, he could have been absent for any number of reasons.

After that breakfast, I learned that Robert Ouko was having a private breakfast with President Bush at the White House. When I learned that, I demanded to know how that event could have taken place without my advance knowledge. The explanation was that Bush and Ouko had become close diplomatic colleagues in the early 1980s when they were both permanent representatives to the United Nations from their respective countries. Bush was like that. When he made friends during his public service, especially in diplomacy, he kept in touch, and invited those friends to call when they came to Washington. Ouko called, and Bush invited him to a private breakfast. It was a meeting of old friends and had nothing to do with US-Kenya bilateral relations.

I did not see Moi after he learned of Ouko's private breakfast at the White House, but I could imagine his fury. Ouko lost his job as foreign minister shortly after Moi returned to Kenya. A few months later, Ouko died under suspicious circumstances while visiting his hometown in western Kenya. The Kenya government asked the UK's Scotland Yard to send an investigator to help determine what caused Ouko's death. The investigator came, and later issued a report that called Ouko's death a homicide and traced the source of the homicide to the Kenyan presidency. Naturally, nothing happened after that, and the case was closed without follow-up.

Flash forward to 2007 and Kenya's presidential elections. The election was marked by severe ethnic violence, including thousands of people killed and tens of thousands displaced from their homes. A leading Kenyan politician, Uhuru Kenyatta, the son of Kenya's founding father Jomo Kenyatta, has come under indictment by the International Criminal Court for his alleged role in the incitement of this violence.

Such is the dilemma of US policy in Africa. How do we cope with the human rights atrocities committed by our best friends? It isn't easy.

Arap Moi's twenty-four years in power were a period when the culturally and economically dominant Kikuyu ethnic group was out of power. In view of their major role in the struggle against British colonialism and the fact that Kikuyu hero Jomo Kenyatta was the founding father, they felt that they were the natural rulers of Kenya. But after Kenyatta's death in 1978, Moi's Kalenjin ethnic group said, "Now it is our turn to eat." The bulk of the fruits of political patronage went to Moi's close associates. Indeed, many Kalenjin intellectuals complained that their ethnic group saw very few material benefits from Moi's presidency, because the wealth was spread so narrowly.

The Kikuyu were able to reclaim the presidency with the election of Mwai Kibaki in 2002. Nevertheless, ethnicity remains an extremely volatile issue in Kenyan politics, and violence continues to be endemic. Moi had the power to do something about ethnic violence, but he did not see the issue as one of his priorities.

From the US point of view, Moi could not have been a more loyal friend.

Secretary of State James A. Baker III (center) and Assistant Secretary of State for Africa Herman J. Cohen (right) meet with Kenneth Kaunda, president of the Republic of Zambia, in Lusaka, 1990.
Credit: USIS Lusaka

CHAPTER 5

Kenneth Kaunda—Zambia

"In the morning he prays. In the afternoon he sings.
In the evening he cries."

Historical Note

Kenneth Kaunda was the founding father and first president of the Republic of Zambia. Under British colonial rule, Zambia was called Northern Rhodesia. An educator in the northern region of Zambia among the Bemba people, Kaunda was the son of a Church of Scotland minister. His father's work took him to different countries in the English-speaking subregion, especially Nyasaland, now Malawi, and Southern Rhodesia, now Zimbabwe.

In the 1950s, Kaunda emulated other intellectual leaders in the British African colonial system by joining political organizations that were agitating for independence. Like his counterparts in Kenya, Tanzania, and Zimbabwe, Kaunda spent some time in British jails for being too zealous in opposing the British crown. As in other countries, prison time in colonial jails made him a national hero. By 1960, Kaunda had risen to the top of the African nationalist movement in Northern Rhodesia and formed his own nationalist party, the United National Independence Party (UNIP). When the British allowed self-government in 1962, he was the clear choice for prime minister. And when full independence came in 1964, he was popularly elected president.

As president, Kaunda's policies were in the intellectual mainstream of his generation. He took the advice of his mentors in the British Labour party and nationalized the commanding heights of the economy, especially the ultra rich copper mining industry, the main source of state revenue. He also agreed with his peers that the

Western multiparty democratic system was incompatible with African culture. He therefore amended the constitution to make UNIP the sole legal party in a single-party system.

The nationalization of the copper industry, combined with the single-party political system, resulted in a decline in the Zambian economy between 1964 and 1990. The copper industry fell into low production under government administrators, and the UNIP party slipped into high corruption. In addition, Kaunda used significant amounts of state resources to support freedom fighters against the white minority regimes in Rhodesia and South Africa and against the Portuguese colonialists in Mozambique and Angola.

Toward the end of the 1980s, Kaunda bowed to internal and international pressure to accept multiparty democracy in Zambia. He believed that UNIP remained popular as the party that brought independence to Zambia and entered a process of free and fair elections in 1991. He and his party suffered unexpected defeat. Labor union leader Frederick Chiluba became Zambia's second president. Kaunda remained in Zambia as a respected elder statesman.

I first had the opportunity to meet President Kaunda in 1965 when I transferred from the American Consulate General in Salisbury, Southern Rhodesia, to the new American Embassy in Lusaka, Zambia. The first American ambassador to the new Republic was Dr. Robert C. Good, professor of international relations at the University of Denver. Bob was one of the main organizers of the "Kennedy for President" campaign in the state of Colorado during the 1960 election. He performed the same service for Lyndon Johnson during the 1964 election. As a specialist in African politics, Good gladly accepted the ambassadorship to Zambia. His previous governmental assignment had been as director of Africa research for the State Department's Bureau of Intelligence and Research.

When my family and I arrived in Lusaka, the country was in a state of tension. The white minority regime in Southern Rhodesia had unilaterally and illegally declared its independence from Britain. The United Kingdom asked the international community to impose drastic economic sanctions against the illegal Rhodesian regime. While Rhodesia was totally cut off from international trade and finance, the white minority *apartheid* regime in the Republic of South Africa came to its rescue. Through their common border flowed trade, aid, and financial products.

Zambia, however, was caught in a trap by the international sanctions against Rhodesia. Oil products, for example, destined for the oil refinery in the city of Umtali in eastern Rhodesia had come through the Mozambique port of Beira, where the pipeline feeding the Umtali refinery received its crude oil. But the British navy blockaded the port. With the refinery closed, the Rhodesians were able to import oil products from South Africa. But Zambia could not. Zambia was left with small and insufficient amounts of oil products available from Malawi and Congo-Zaire. Gasoline had to be rationed at the rate of four gallons per month per vehicle.

Because of sanctions, Zambia could not export its copper, amounting to four hundred thousand tons per year, through the normal rail route passing through Rhodesia en route to the port of Laurenço Marques in Mozambique. In short, when I arrived in Lusaka to take up my position as economic-commercial officer at the US Embassy, Zambia was in a state of crisis. Going to the office every day, I had a choice of riding my bike or being picked up by the embassy station wagon. I did not get enough gas for my own car to do more than weekend shopping.

As a liberal Democrat, Ambassador Good was a great admirer of the African founding fathers who led their liberation movements. He was particularly fond of Kenneth Kaunda, fondly known to his people as KK, and the feeling was mutual. For that reason, Ambassador Good and staff members like myself had plenty of face time with Kaunda.

Kaunda wore Zambia's economic hardship as a badge of honor. Just as the black majorities in Rhodesia, Angola, Mozambique, and South Africa were suffering from oppression, Zambians suffered, too. While Kaunda's foreign policy was "nonaligned" or neutral between the Soviet Union and the United States, he saw the United States as the main hope for ending racial oppression in southern Africa. Needless to say, he identified heavily with the Kennedy-Johnson administration.

In our meetings, Kaunda was cordial and intellectually astute.

He believed that the whites in Rhodesia and South Africa and the Portuguese colonialists in Mozambique and Angola would eventually come to their senses. In the meantime, he expected US support for the "liberation struggle." In contrast to Kenya's second president, Daniel Arap Moi, for example, who was quite stiff, Kaunda was totally relaxed with foreign visitors. His favorite act of hospitality was to pour tea for his visitors with no household servants in sight.

In those tense days, the United States did come to Zambia's aid in a number of ways in order to assure vital imports and exports. For example, we arranged for Zambia to purchase used Lockheed Hercules cargo aircraft from Alaska Airlines. These aircraft, with American crews, were able to airlift extremely heavy copper ingots for an interim period while road transport links through the port of Dar es Salaam were being established. We also arranged for a one-time airlift of oil products from Congo-Zaire in US Air Force cargo planes.

The key to Zambia's logistical independence was surface transport through Tanzania to the port of Dar es Salaam. In the Embassy, we debated the two options, road or rail. Washington, through USAID, was committed to providing the necessary funding. We finally came down on the side of building the road. The rail option was determined to be economically unfeasible. We started building the road in 1967, while the Chinese decided to contribute to the liberation struggle by building the railway.

As a result of my frequent encounters with Kaunda accompanying Ambassador Good, Kaunda remembered me favorably, and I was able to have access whenever I needed it. This came in handy when I became assistant secretary of state in 1989, and Kaunda was in an important position to help in conflict mediation in Angola and Mozambique.

I moved on to Kinshasa, Congo-Zaire, after departing Lusaka in late 1996. During one of my conversations with President Mobutu, I asked him his opinion about some of the other leaders in Africa, especially the English-speaking intellectual crowd in the east and south. During one conversation, I said, "Marshall, what do you think of Julius Nyerere, president of Tanzania, and Kenneth Kaunda, president of Zambia. Congo-Zaire has long borders with both countries. "

Mobutu was normally in awe of his elders among African heads of state. He considered Houphouët-Boigny of Côte d'Ivoire to be his spiritual father. He was very fond of President Tombalbaye of Chad, a former schoolteacher, and was on the phone almost every day schmoozing with President Eyadema of Togo, a military dictator like himself. He considered President Senghor of Senegal to be one of the great intellectual leaders of Africa along with the king of Morocco.

But when it came to Nyerere and Kaunda, Mobutu saw two phonies. In response to my question, Mobutu said, "I detest Nyerere and Kaunda."

"Why is that Marshall?"

"The international community, especially you Americans, loves Nyerere. He pretends to be a great intellectual. He translated Shakespeare's play *Julius Caesar* into Swahili. But how many political prisoners does he have? Human rights activists are always attacking me. Nyerere has over 1,500 political prisoners. I don't have any. I co-opt my political opponents."

"What about Kaunda?"

Mobutu laughed. "In the morning, Kaunda prays. In the afternoon, Kaunda laughs. In the evening, Kaunda cries." He tries to look like a compassionate leader, but his political opponents, as well as his political associates who become too independent, tend to disappear regularly. How many politicians are living in exile?"

As a matter of fact, Kaunda was known to shed tears in public and did spend a certain amount of time offering prayers. But when it came to internal politics, he could be ruthless against any Zambian who expressed opposing views. His public image, on the other hand, was one of compassion and understanding. Visiting Americans ate that up.

In general, our relations with Kaunda revolved around the southern African liberation saga. While he criticized US engagement with the South African government as "immoral and unacceptable," especially during Republican administrations, he never refused to listen to our proposals and analysis with respect and understanding.

I found Kaunda to be particularly helpful when we were trying to establish negotiating processes in both Angola and Mozambique.

The presidents of both countries were initially reluctant to accept the idea of negotiating with rebel groups they considered to be surrogates of enemies in the west. In Mozambique, President Chissano and his Central Committee in the ruling FRELIMO party considered the rebel group RENAMO to be pure surrogates of the intelligence service of white South Africa. In Angola, President Dos Santos and his ruling MPLA party had the same view of the rebel group UNITA. They both expected the United States to force South Africa to stop supporting the two rebel groups. They refused to accord any degree of legitimacy to RENAMO or UNITA as representing a certain segment of their respective societies.

Kaunda told me that he was very close to both Chissano of Mozambique and Dos Santos of Angola. He agreed with President Bush that the rebels had legitimate support in the countryside and needed to be coaxed into regular political life. He also reminded me that UNITA president Savimbi used to be big on the Lusaka cocktail party circuit when he was fighting the Portuguese out of northwest Zambia. Looking back at our efforts in both Mozambique and Angola, I conclude that Kaunda was quite helpful in the initiation of two peace processes.

While Kaunda was a strong contributor to peace in southern Africa, he was a loser when it came to domestic affairs in Zambia. The copper industry, exporting 400,000 tons a year, went into a steep decline because of corrupt government administrators connected to the ruling party. Agricultural production fell sharply because farm-to-market roads were not maintained. In general, poverty levels rose sharply during Kaunda's twenty-seven years in power. While all of this was going on, Kaunda was busy on the international circuit fighting for the liberation of southern Africa.

With the Cold War over by 1990, Kaunda was feeling both internal and external pressure to end the single-party monopoly and bring about a transition to multiparty democracy, starting with a free and fair competitive election. Feeling totally confident that the Zambian people still revered him, Kaunda agreed to modify the constitution to allow for the existence of multiple political parties. He also scheduled a presidential election.

The main opposition party that arose immediately after the constitution was changed was called the Movement for Multiparty

Democracy (MMD). In reality, the movement had existed unofficially for several years before it could begin operating legitimately. The leadership was made up of a younger generation of university-educated Zambians who saw the need to get rid of the corruption of a monopoly party in power, as well as the need to bring about economic reforms. The standard bearer for the presidential election was Frederick Chiluba, the president of the Zambian Mineworkers Union.

The election was certified as being free and fair by independent observers and ended with a victory by Frederick Chiluba. I was visiting Botswana, to the immediate southwest of Zambia, when the election results were announced. I flew at once to Lusaka to visit both the winner and the loser. While awaiting a signal to fly to Ndola in the copper mining region to see President-elect Chiluba, I called on Kaunda in Lusaka. As expected, I found him quite despondent. He was in despair for Zambia. He was expecting that tragedy would strike his beloved country. His first statement to me was, "They have elected a bunch of drug dealers."

I could not quite understand what Kaunda was talking about when he mentioned drug dealers. Nevertheless, I assured him that his wise counsel would still be needed as we sought to find solutions in Angola and Mozambique.

I then visited Chiluba, who was surrounded by ebullient young advisers anxious to start moving on reform of the Zambian government. I told Chiluba that it was important for him to pay tribute to Kaunda for allowing democracy to work. He promised to do that. He also informed me that his government would be assisting UNITA leader Jonas Savimbi against the Angolan government. Savimbi and his movement had close ethnic ties in Northern Zambia, where all of the popular sentiment was on his side.

Later, I asked Zambian friends about Kaunda's remark regarding drug dealers allegedly within the newly elected MMD party. I was informed that there was a network of amphetamine drugs being trafficked to the Republic of South Africa via Zambia and that one prominent individual in the MMD was implicated. Later, after I retired from the Foreign Service, I heard that the State Department was warning the president of Zambia not to appoint this individual to the position of foreign minister if it wanted to have cordial relations with the United States.

But for that one individual allegedly involved in drug trafficking, the MMD did a credible job governing Zambia after Kaunda lost the election. It took Kaunda a while to get over his loss, but he later recovered to take on the role of respected elder statesman. Like many of his peers, Kaunda in power had become the prisoner of a corrupt system that he himself had unwittingly established.

President Robert Mugabe of the Republic of Zimbabwe at a conference in
The Netherlands in 1998.
Credit: en.wikipedia.org

CHAPTER 6

Robert Mugabe — Zimbabwe

Marxism-Leninism Forever

Historical Note

As a young university graduate from British Southern Rhodesia, Robert Mugabe experienced the independence of Ghana in 1957 and became an adherent of African nationalism and Marxist ideology as propagated by Kwame Nkrumah, independent Ghana's founding father and first president. Upon his return from Ghana to Rhodesia, he became caught up in the black majority's struggle for majority rule.

The nationalist movement was divided between the two major African ethnic nations—the Ndebele and the Shona. Mugabe joined the Zimbabwe African National Union (ZANU) and quickly rose to the top leadership. He spent ten years in prison for his activities. Released in 1975, he made his way to Mozambique, where the newly independent African regime allowed him to organize armed resistance to the white regime in Rhodesia across the border. The Rhodesian war lasted until 1980, when the South African, British, and American governments applied pressure on the white minority rulers in Rhodesia to begin the negotiations that resulted in majority rule and a new name for the country, Zimbabwe.

Mugabe was elected the first prime minister in recognition of his effective guerrilla leadership. His first twenty years as Zimbabwe's leader were constructive, tolerant, and prosperous. Toward the beginning of the twenty-first century, Mugabe realized that he was losing popularity and risking electoral defeat. As a confirmed Marxist-Leninist, Mugabe was determined to keep his ZANU party in power. Losing an election was not an option. The result was the decline of Zimbabwe through confiscation of white-owned commercial farmland, the loss of agricultural production, a steep decline of GNP, and the deepening poverty of a once prosperous middle class, which emigrated to South Africa in large numbers. For Mugabe, staying in power has been all that counts. He celebrated his 89th birthday in March 2013, fully expecting to win the next election. The thugs in his ZANU-PF party were ready to guarantee the necessary intimidation of voters to insure a rigged election. In August 2013 Mugabe won his seventh term as president.

It was September 1988. The United Nations General Assembly General Debate was in full swing. As I walked through the hall of the General Assembly building with Secretary of State George Shultz, I said, "I ran into Robert Mugabe, president of Zimbabwe, a few hours ago. He wants to see you."

Shultz's face reddened. "Absolutely not. Keep him away from me. He is constantly lecturing about issues that should not concern him. He wants us to stop helping the anti-Soviet rebels in Afghanistan. He is a nonaligned nag."

Flash forward to January 1991. "Desert Storm," the first Gulf War, was still ongoing. Zimbabwe had just joined the UN Security Council as a non-permanent member for a two-year rotational tour. President George H. W. Bush was sensitive to Security Council voting about the war. During August 1990, Secretary of State James Baker instructed me to make sure that the three African members of the Security Council voted in favor of going to war against Iraq. I succeeded in persuading Zaire, Ethiopia, and Côte d'Ivoire to vote with the United States for the crucial war resolution in August.

With Zimbabwe replacing Côte d'Ivoire in January 1991, we were concerned that President Mugabe, a good friend and collaborator of Iraq's president Saddam Hussein in the Non-Aligned Movement, would demonstrate hostility to the international military action to liberate Kuwait from Iraqi occupation.

I decided to visit Mugabe, whom I had known since he became Zimbabwe's first president in 1980. Making flight reservations, I was informed by State Department security that I could not travel through the usual European route. Saddam had unleashed his many terrorist friends to attack American interests in Europe, Africa, and beyond. My only option was to fly to Brazil, and then across the south Atlantic to Johannesburg, South Africa, and then north to Harare, the capital of Zimbabwe.

Accompanied by my executive assistant, Karl Hoffman, I arrived at Mugabe's office with some trepidation. In view of his Non-Aligned leadership, I expected to be thoroughly harangued. I made my pitch and waited for Mugabe's hammer.

He thought for a while and then made a response that blew me away: "Secretary Cohen, I don't approve of strong powers invading and occupying weaker powers. Iraq must be forced out of Kuwait. Tell President Bush that I am fully on his side on this question."

Wow! That was an unexpected surprise. Walking out of Mugabe's presidential office complex, I said to Karl Hoffman, "That was too good to be true. Let's take tomorrow off and visit Victoria Falls."

Mugabe was true to his word. Shortly after our visit, Iraqi agents slipped into Zimbabwe and set up in a hotel with a direct line of sight to the American Embassy. They were preparing to kill the US ambassador. Zimbabwe intelligence spotted them upon arrival, followed and surveilled them, and then arrested them. The Zimbabwe service sent them to Cyprus to American counterparts for interrogation.

American diplomats generally found Mugabe a reasonable interlocutor between 1980, when he became president, and the year 2000, when his internal policies became totally radical and Zimbabwe started a steady decent into economic and political chaos. British diplomats presiding over majority rule and independence negotiations in 1979 found Mugabe to be moderate and pragmatic. American diplomats who observed those talks said the same thing.

Like South Africa, Zimbabwe was under white minority rule for over half a century. While South Africa achieved full independence from Great Britain in 1912, Zimbabwe remained a British crown colony as Southern Rhodesia between 1928 and 1980. The colony had been granted self-rule in 1928. This allowed the white minority to keep the black majority totally subjugated, since the Africans had no voting rights. The Rhodesian system of segregation was a bit less harsh than the South African *apartheid* system, but the blacks felt totally repressed nevertheless.

Beginning in 1957 with Ghana, the British started granting independence to its African colonies. In 1964, Northern Rhodesia and Nyasaland gained independence as Zambia and Malawi, respectively. These developments in Southern Rhodesia's immediate neighborhood stirred up both white and black citizens. The whites felt that their country was far more advanced economically than the newly independent states and demanded equal treatment. The blacks demanded that the United Kingdom refuse independence until majority rule under democracy could be negotiated.

These two opposing views of independence had a profound impact on Rhodesian politics. The white community became more radicalized and extremist, as passions for independence intensified. Within the black community, passions for equal rights and majority rule gave rise to a strong political movement that the whites saw as subversive and dangerous.

Within this heated political context, Robert Mugabe became a leading advocate for equal rights and majority rule. A university graduate with a degree in education, Mugabe was completing his graduate studies in Ghana in 1960 shortly after that British colony achieved independence in 1957. Mugabe came under the influence of Ghana's first president, Kwame Nkrumah, a leader of significant charisma. Nkrumah's message was, "Marxism and African unity." From that moment, Mugabe started down the road toward full acceptance of Marxist ideology as interpreted by Lenin.

When Mugabe returned to Rhodesia in 1961, he found a full-fledged black nationalist movement in an expansion mode under a popular and charismatic leader, Joshua Nkomo. Mugabe's message had an ideological element that appealed to educated blacks looking for an alternative to Nkomo, who lacked intellectual weight. In addition, Nkomo came from the minority Ndebele ethnic group. Mugabe was part of the majority Shona group. The result was two competing nationalist movements that weakened the overall quest for majority rule.

When I arrived in Rhodesia in late 1963 on assignment to the American consulate general, Mugabe was in jail serving a ten-year sentence for subversion. My job was to meet with black political leaders. While I was able to see Nkomo, president of the Zimbabwe African Peoples Union (ZAPU), I was not allowed to see Mugabe in prison. Nkomo's message was, "When will the United States give us our majority rule?" In other words, you can put pressure on the United Kingdom, the colonial power. Mugabe's followers, in his Zimbabwe African National Union (ZANU), talked to me about the inevitable revolution. Hatred between the two organizations was strong.

In 1965, the white minority regime unilaterally declared independence for Rhodesia in defiance of the UK colonial power, which imposed full economic sanctions, including an oil blockade. This set the stage for an inevitable armed conflict. In 1977, Mugabe was authorized to attend a conference in Zambia. Instead of returning, he slipped into independent Mozambique, where he started an armed insurgency against the illegal white regime. Nkomo and his party joined the insurgency from a separate base in Zambia. The only country willing to allow Rhodesian trade to transit its territory was *apartheid* South Africa.

The war lasted three years. During that period, the ZANU operation was the more successful in penetrating deep into the Rhodesian countryside, causing great havoc among the white commercial farmers. Working from across the Zambezi River in Zambia, the ZAPU insurgency was relatively feeble. Hence, the black population of Rhodesia saw ZANU in action far more often than ZAPU.

In 1979, under pressure from the *apartheid* government of South Africa, the white minority regime of Southern Rhodesia agreed to negotiate a transition to black majority rule. The negotiation took place in December 1979 at Lancaster House in London. The conference wrote a new constitution and arranged for democratic elections. White Rhodesians were guaranteed ten percent of the seats in the new parliament, and a ten-year period of land reform was initiated. This was designed to purchase land from white commercial farmers in order to resettle landless black farmers.

Because Mugabe's ZANU was so much more effective and visible in the war against the white regime, his party easily won the first democratic election, and he became the first prime minister of Zimbabwe, the country's new name.

Under the influence of Nkrumah of Ghana and his lengthy

reading of Marxist literature during his ten years in prison, Mugabe took over the political leadership of Zimbabwe as a confirmed Marxist-Leninist. That meant, above all, that the vanguard peoples' party would guide the nation to full socialism. ZANU, therefore, would remain supreme and permanently in power. As a result, Zimbabwe's laws were written and amended so that ZANU would become the only legal political party.

During the 1990s, visitors to Harare, Zimbabwe's capital, saw that the real political and governmental action took place not in the halls of the bureaucracy but at ZANU headquarters, standing on its own plaza in the heart of downtown. All major policy decisions were made there by the party's political bureau.

Between 1980 and 2000, Zimbabwe was an economic and political leader in Africa. High agricultural production was a big money earner. Its Virginia tobacco exports were second only to the United States. Zimbabwe maize was exported to most southern African countries.

One of my most important discussions with Mugabe in the early 1990s concerned the civil war in Mozambique. During that country's guerrilla war of 1976–1979, the Rhodesians had financed and armed a guerrilla force against the independent African regime in Mozambique. This was done in retaliation for the Mozambican support to Mugabe and his fighters.

After the beginning of peace in Zimbabwe, the Mozambique guerilla war continued. After Mugabe became the political leader in Zimbabwe, the white *apartheid* regime in South Africa took over support of the anti-regime guerrillas in Mozambique, known as RENAMO. In the State Department, we felt that the Mozambique war was ripe for mediation toward a democratic transition.

We embarked on a number of initiatives that led to progress. But the most difficult problem was to persuade the RENAMO leader, Alphonse Dhlakama, to accept the prospect of laying down his weapons and participating in a democratic process. His paranoia was great, and he fully expected to be killed by the Mozambique military if he entered political life.

I had a number of secret meetings with Dhlakama in Malawi, but I was never able to fully persuade him to accept negotiations and subsequent entry into political life. The person who accomplished this was Robert Mugabe. I asked Mugabe to undertake this task because he and Dhlakama came from the same Shona ethnic group that straddles the Zimbabwe-Mozambique border. Mugabe succeeded where many of us failed, and in May 1992 in Rome, he presided over the signing of the Mozambique peace accords. As of early 2013, Dhlakama continued to be active in Mozambique politics as an opposition leader.

In view of his reasonable and helpful cooperation on foreign relations, and his moderate and ostensibly pro-market policies at home, how did Mugabe become so irrational and destructive after the beginning of the 21st century?

I started to suspect something was going wrong when I sat about five feet away from Mugabe at the annual summit meeting of the Global Coalition for Africa in November 1995, in the conference center in Maastricht, Netherlands. I was a senior advisor to the GCA, an intergovernmental forum designed to bring donor countries and African countries to a consensus on the correct economic policies to promote development.

In his plenary address, Mugabe made an impassioned plea for the international community to prevent African countries from abandoning democracy. It was a period when most African countries were experimenting with multiparty democracy after several decades of one-party authoritarian rule. By the time of the conference, some of the African countries were beginning to slip backwards from their democracy toward a return to authoritarianism.

Mugabe's plea for the sustainability of democracy was elegant and heart warming. But after he completed his oration, he continued on with another, totally irrelevant, subject that made us all gasp. He started a rant against homosexuality that he considered a total abomination. The sentence that has stayed in my memory ever since was: "How is it possible for us to allow a man to make another man into a woman?"

Fortunately, Chairman Jan Pronk, then labor minister of the Netherlands, gaveled Mugabe to a close with "I am sorry Mr. President, but your time is up." We all looked astonished. Needless to say, word of Mugabe's rant leaked out to the public. The gay community quickly organized an anti-Mugabe demonstration.

During the second half of the 1990s, Mugabe's popularity started to decline. His government had done an excellent job of providing basic education to the youth. But his Marxist ideology caused him to be suspicious of the private sector, thereby discouraging new private investment. The result was a huge influx of high school and university graduates into the labor market, with very few jobs available. When I visited Harare in 1998, ordinary people working in hotels, stores, and restaurants were quite open in expressing their fatigue with Mugabe.

Mugabe tried to restore his popularity through the expropriation of commercial farmland owned by white farmers. He first demanded that the United Kingdom finance the purchase of land for the benefit of African farmers, as they had done shortly after Zimbabwe's independence under black majority rule. The UK government refused to start a new program of land purchases, claiming that the earlier program had benefited political elites and not the landless rural peasants.

In a desperate effort to stimulate a feeling of nationalism, Mugabe unleashed his ZANU party thugs onto white-owned farmland, resulting in severe hardship to the white farmers and great damage to the Zimbabwe economy. A once great exporter of maize and Virginia tobacco went into deep decline. Mugabe, one of the most important African freedom fighters, was becoming an international pariah.

Mugabe's rallying cry was, "Our lands were illegally stolen by the whites one hundred years ago." The truth of the matter was that the majority of white-owned farms had been purchased after he had been elected prime minister in 1980. The expatriate farmers had confidence in Mugabe's moderation and respect for property. After all, he had appointed a white Zimbabwean minister of agriculture.

My last private conversation with Mugabe took place in the year 2000 in the midst of the farm confiscations. He had asked me to advise him about what he could do to reverse the economic decline. He did not want to get into the farm issue. I told him I would develop an economic stabilization plan for him and suggested that he try to link up with the World Bank and the IMF for financial assistance based on needed policy reforms. During that conversation, he was perfectly rational and showed no sign of hysteria about what was going on around him in the countryside.

Some say that the loss of his first wife, Sally, and his second marriage to Grace Marufu were important factors in his change of outlook. His first wife, a Ghanaian, was deeply interested in social development. His second wife was apparently interested mostly in the accumulation of wealth. My own view is that Mugabe was driven mainly by his deep adherence to Marxism-Leninism. This doctrine taught him that the vanguard party, the ZANU-PF party in his case, must never give up power. In the late 1990s, it was clear that his party would eventually lose out in free and fair elections. He had to do everything possible to forestall the loss of power. Hence, he resorted to the farm confiscations, electoral intimidations, and sheer brutality in the tradition of Lenin and Stalin.

Many years later, I talked to some of my retired colleagues who had known Mugabe in the early 1960s, when he was an aspiring political leader. They told me that his only interest was political power. He expressed no interest in economic development, land ownership, or any bread and butter issues. He cared only for power, as a devoted Leninist would.

As of the beginning of 2014, Zimbabwe was still in the throes of disaster, as the Mugabe regime continued to flounder in corruption and repression. Mugabe, in his upper eighties, appeared to be under the control of military and high political cronies. Zimbabwe awaited his departure with impatience.

From an Africa-wide perspective, Zimbabwe presents an extreme example of the one-party state that acts as a drag on economic development, among other reasons. The party-state is full of careerists who have few expectations for employment opportunities in the private sector. Thus, apart from Leninist theories about the "vanguard party," keeping the party in power is the highest political priority. One ameliorating phenomenon is the constitutional two-term mandate for some heads of state, as in Tanzania, Zambia, and Mali. While the party remains in power, the required turnover of heads of state every eight years sets up a competitive dynamic within the party that has some democratic aspects. As Zimbabwe's economy has plunged since the year 2000 and as Mugabe's heirs see themselves inheriting less and less, maneuvering for power within the ZANU party has become more intense.

Tragedies such as the one perpetrated by Mugabe and his ZANU party also have an impact on the surrounding region. Zimbabwe used to be a regional breadbasket, especially for maize, the staple food of most southern African populations. The decline of maize production in Zimbabwe has caused the price of this staple to rise in the Congo, Zambia, Mozambique, and Angola.

One irony that must be gnawing on Mugabe is the way neighboring countries have welcomed Zimbabwe's white farmers with open arms. Those who are still willing to give Africa a second chance are doing well as commercial farmers in Zambia, Mozambique, and even in some places in Nigeria; while back in Zimbabwe, most of the former commercial farms are now home to African peasant farmers who cannot get title to the land because of Mugabe's Marxist policies. Without land titles, they cannot obtain bank credit and are thus condemned to remain subsistence farmers.

As of early 2015, Zimbabwe was still in the throes of disaster, as the Mugabe regime continued to flounder in corruption and repression. Mugabe, at age 90, seemed still to be under the control of military and high political cronies. But in October 2014, Mugabe's wife Grace suddenly entered politics as chairperson of the ZANU Women's League. From this position, Grace began to make statements that she expected to succeed to the presidency after her husband's demise. This added to the impatience of the Zimbabwe people to see the end of the Mugabes. Any effort to make Grace the ZANU-PF candidate for president will unite all factions against her.

Will Zimbabwe start back on the road to good governance after Mugabe? In my view, with or without Mugabe, ZANU-PF will break up into competing factions. It will be military against civilians and a free-for-all among different groups within the party, each one following a different senior leader considered the legitimate heir apparent. A military takeover would not be surprising. The medium-term prognosis for Zimbabwe as of early 2015 was bleak. Mugabe may be Africa's last true-believing Marxist-Leninist.

GROUP III

The Congolese:
Oh Belgium! What have you wrought?

The late president of the Republic of Zaire, Mobutu Sese Seko, and Mrs. Mobutu (left) with the State Department's director of Central African affairs, Herman J. Cohen, and Mrs. Cohen at a White House dinner in March 1970.
Credit: White House photo

CHAPTER 7

Joseph Désiré Mobutu—Zaire

Mobutu Sese Seko Nkuku Ngbendu
wa za Banga

Historical Note

Born to a modest family in the far north of the Belgian Congo, Joseph Désiré Mobutu was noticed by his elementary Catholic schoolteachers as a young person with intelligence and good prospects. They encouraged him to pursue higher education. He came of age in the late 1950s, just as the Belgian government was preparing to grant independence to its giant colony in Africa. Mobutu went to Belgium to pursue journalism studies in 1957. He also took military training. When Congo's independence took place on June 30, 1960, the country was totally unprepared. There were only a handful of university graduates, and there had been no training for self-government. In Belgium, Mobutu joined intellectual circles and became active in Congolese politics. After his return, he joined the colonial Force Publique, the paramilitary group that was to become the independent Congolese army. He was an enlisted man because Africans could not become officers.

After independence, disorder was widespread. Congolese troops mutinied against their Belgian officers. The political system was torn between pro-Western and pro-Soviet factions. Ethnic animosities played a role in creating chaos. Belgian business interests sought to persuade provincial political leaders in the mineral-producing provinces to secede. The US government decided that only a UN peacekeeping operation could restore order, and the UN Security Council voted to approve such an operation. UN troops and civil servants from many nations maintained stability from 1960 to 1968.

In 1965, as the best-educated and highest-ranking enlisted man, Mobutu had advanced to become the commanding general of the Congolese army. In view of the general political and administrative chaos in all parts of the country, Mobutu decided to stage a coup d'état and take power. There are reliable reports that Mobutu had the support of the Central Intelligence Agency of the United States to make this move.

During his early years as head of state, Mobutu was quite friendly with the United States and followed American advice regarding economic reforms. These were successful until problems developed in 1975. As he grew more secure in his position of supreme leader, he became increasingly independent of American influence, although he was careful to maintain close ties with all US administrations. After the onset of profound economic problems in 1975, Mobutu's administration became increasingly corrupt and isolated. His "pro-West" international policies kept him in good graces with the United States and Europe, which continued to provide substantial aid. After 1990, however, international support dwindled.

In 1996, Mobutu was unable to defend his regime against rebels who began combat operations at the eastern edge of the country, supported by the governments of Rwanda and Uganda. That same year he retreated to Morocco, where he died of prostate cancer in 1997. During his thirty-one years in power, his country was relatively stable. Since his departure, the Congo has been increasingly unstable. The irony is that Mobutu's departure from power made most Congolese happy. Since that time, the Congo's chronic instability has caused many Congolese to say, "Life under Mobutu was better than at any time since his demise."

❖ ❖ ❖

In 1972, seven years after taking power in a military coup, Mobutu decreed that all citizens must discard their Western Christian first names and adopt African names. This was part of his overall strategy to downplay Western culture and take his people back to their African roots. Five years earlier, he had changed the country's name from Republic of the Congo to Zaire, and the name of the capital city from Léopoldville to Kinshasa.

Translations of Mobutu's adopted African name vary. The official one was "the all-powerful warrior who goes from conquest to conquest leaving fire in his wake." This version stimulated guffaws both within and outside the country. The underground translation making the rounds of Kinshasa and Washington was "the all-powerful rooster who leaves no hen intact."

Despite his international reputation for buffoonery and for power going to his head, those of us in the international community, both governmental and private, who dealt with Mobutu on a regular basis, found him quite rational and relatively sophisticated, at least during his earlier years in power.

My first official encounter with him in 1967 involved his nationalization of the country's copper industry. The Belgian-owned mines in the southern province of Katanga were producing 400,000 tons of refined copper annually. They were the lifeblood of the nation—the crown jewels. As a number of other new African heads of state had decided before him, Mobutu felt that his country could not be truly independent until the major source of wealth came under Zaire's sovereign ownership.

When Mobutu made the announcement of the nationalization of Union Minière du Haut Katanga (UMHK), the subsidiary of the Belgian conglomerate Société Générale, he enjoyed tremendous popularity within the intellectual class. Students from the Lovanium University came down from the hills surrounding Kinshasa to march in the streets singing Mobutu's praises. I had the feeling watching them that they were genuine and had not been bribed into demonstrating. His gesture of anticolonial economic nationalism had struck a popular chord.

Unfortunately, Mobutu also announced that his government would not pay compensation to the Belgian owners, arguing that the Belgians had siphoned off the country's wealth for over a century. Compensation was out of the question. This was an unambiguous violation of international law. Belgium went to the World Bank with a request that all international assistance to Zaire be suspended immediately. The World Bank and all the other donors complied. Mobutu was out on a limb because his government was heavily dependent on foreign aid.

As chargé d'affaires at the American Embassy at the time, I

went to see Mobutu to discuss the problem. He listened calmly, complaining that none of his advisors knew enough about the issue to warn him. But he could not backtrack on compensation. He would become a laughingstock if he agreed to pay compensation after all of his nationalistic anti-Belgian rhetoric. He asked the embassy to come up with a solution. After some brainstorming in our economic section, we concluded that the copper mines had to have expatriate management until Congolese could be trained. There would have to be a transition to enable Zairians to become educated and trained to take over. An interim international management team would have to be hired. We proposed that one of the Belgian companies in the former ownership conglomerate take the management contract. The fee could be sufficiently inflated to provide for hidden compensation.

We saw that World Bank president Robert McNamara was coming to Kinshasa specifically to discuss the nationalization issue. He felt that one of Africa's largest and most important countries could not be deprived of development assistance. I briefed McNamara on our idea and proposed that he be the one to sell it to Mobutu. McNamara agreed, and Mobutu accepted it. My conclusion was that despite his public foolishness, Mobutu was capable of behaving like a pragmatic adult.

For his initial years in power, Mobutu felt he must demonstrate that he was diminishing Belgian economic and political power. After all, there had been no nationalist struggle before independence. Belgian rule just collapsed. Mobutu needed to initiate and complete the liberation struggle after independence.

As an encore to the copper nationalization in 1967, Mobutu instructed his official political party, the MPR (Popular Movement for the Revolution) to stage a demonstration in front of the Belgian Embassy. It took place on a steamy afternoon. Lots of windows were broken, and lots of Belgian Embassy vehicles were burned. When they finished their anti-Belgian demonstration, the mob noted that the US Embassy was only two blocks away. All "imperialists" look alike. They turned toward us and started throwing rocks at our windows. When about a hundred demonstrators arrived at our front door threatening to break in, the US Marine Guards loaded their weapons. Ambassador Robert McBride, fresh from his previous job as deputy chief of mission in Paris and suffering from a bit of culture shock, called Mobutu on his private phone. Within five minutes, Mobutu arrived, standing in an open Jeep and shooing the party militants away. They dispersed quickly. McBride thanked Mobutu and asked about the flames still visible at the Belgian Embassy. Mobutu sighed and said: "I told them not to do too much damage. They need more training."

In mid-1967, the acting CIA station chief, Frank Jeton, was departing on transfer. Knowing Mobutu's close personal relationship with the CIA station, especially with former chief Larry Devlin, the man most responsible for Mobutu's rise to power, Ambassador McBride decided to invite Mobutu to a farewell dinner for Jeton. Mobutu never accepted embassy invitations, but for Jeton he broke the rule and said yes. Before sitting down to dinner, Mobutu and his close associates were having cocktails on the terrace overlooking the Congo River downstream from Kinshasa, with the city lights of Brazzaville opposite. Mobutu pointed downriver where there were no lights. It was essentially pristine. He said, "I will make sure there will be no development there. We must protect the environment and preserve the riverbanks." He had clearly been doing some reading.

Throughout his presidency, Mobutu straddled two worlds— the traditional African village culture and Western ways. Until about 1975, he managed to move between the two systems with alacrity. After that year, the African side increasingly dominated and eventually led to his loss of perspective.

Mobutu's acceptance of Western methodology underpinning economic development was initially quite promising. On the advice of the American embassy and the United Nations mission, Mobutu accepted a program of economic stabilization designed by the International Monetary Fund in 1967. It was one of the first of its kind in Africa and worked as planned for the first five years. Inflation was brought way down. A new currency, called the Zaire, was created and became convertible in international markets. Stores started to fill up with a variety of imported products. A few supermarkets were opened in the capital city. Foreign development assistance was substantial.

On the negative side of the ledger, Mobutu found it necessary to acquiesce to African tradition. First of all, you take care of your relatives and tribal kinfolk and make sure that the home subregion gets lots of government money. The payrolls of government-owned entities were inflated to the point of negative balance sheets. For example, the World Bank hired American engineer Robert Keating, a graduate of the Massachusetts Institute of Technology, to be director general of public works. Keating quickly discovered that there were three times as many employees on the payroll as the number actually showing up to work every morning. He went to see Mobutu, assuming naively that the president would want to correct this anomaly once it was pointed out to him. Mobutu thanked Keating and then explained that he could not remain in power if he fired all those fictitious workers.

With the economy growing nicely, and with the currency stabilized, Mobutu started to think big. Government revenue from copper exports was substantial at $1.40 per pound. But most of it was eaten up in inflated payrolls, government subsidies to loss-making enterprises, and overall corruption. There was not much left for capital expenditures. With his internal power increasingly secure, apart from some low-level insurgency in the east along the border with Tanzania, Mobutu wanted Zaire to project an international image commensurate with its gigantic size and abundant natural resources. What could he do without big money?

Fortunately for Mobutu, but unfortunately for the country, New York and London were awash with money from high oil prices, especially during the period 1970–1973. Sovereign debt for the developing world had become fashionable. Who could imagine that sovereign governments might default on their debts? Above all, commodity prices were high. The post–World War Two boom continued to keep prices up, especially for African agriculture and minerals. There was built-in collateral for loans.

Mobutu's first order of business was to build a world-class international airline, Air Zaire. Sales people from Boeing and McDonald Douglas, the two big American aircraft manufacturers, were welcomed. With bank loans guaranteed by the U.S. Export-Import Bank, Mobutu could choose his fleet as if he were buying candy. Contrary to all good sense, Mobutu bought large passenger airliners from both companies. Air Zaire was born, and international flights to Brussels and Paris started up. There were also flights to major African cities such as Dakar, Nairobi, Kampala, Abidjan, and Johannesburg.

I was in charge of Zaire affairs at the State Department during 1970–1974 and tried to dissuade Mobutu from buying aircraft from two different companies, in view of the increased problems and costs of maintenance. Both Mobutu and the American companies bit my head off for violating Zairian sovereignty and "undermining" US exports.

Mobutu's second big idea was linked to one of the world's most important down-rushing water sites and its substantial hydroelectric potential. The phenomenon is called Inga and is located on the Congo River about seventy miles from the Atlantic coast. Mobutu wanted to install a hydroelectric dam at Inga, and he wanted to build a thousand-mile transmission line to provide power to the copper mines in Katanga province. The installation of a clean, low-cost power source was a no-brainer in terms of economic development. But the building of a long-distance power line to Katanga made absolutely no sense. Mobutu's motivation was political. He knew that his main political opposition resided there. During the country's early troubles immediately after independence, Katanga's political leadership had been openly talking about secession. Why should they have to share all that copper wealth with the rest of the country? The secessionist movement was defeated by United Nations peacekeepers, but secessionist sentiment remained.

In 1970, President Richard Nixon invited Mobutu to make a state visit to the United States. It was a big event and included a formal arrival at the White House, with marching bands and review of troops. A formal state dinner with over a hundred distinguished guests from government, the business community, and the cultural world topped it off. In two long meetings with President Nixon, Mobutu pitched his ideas for big projects and requested assistance with funding. In addition to his commercial aircraft and Inga dam projects, Mobutu wanted to purchase military cargo aircraft, specifically the Lockheed Hercules C-130. He also asked for a coast guard cutter for Lake Tanganyika and for the latest state-of-the-art jet fighter plane, the U.S. Air Force F-4.

Nixon said yes to everything except the F-4 jet fighters. In a public statement during Mobutu's visit, Nixon said, "The Congo is a good place for business." He urged the American private sector to take a good look at the Congo as an investment destination. This triggered a small flow of business people to my desk as the officer in charge of Congolese affairs at the State Department. I gave the business community a positive briefing on the pro-business atmosphere in the Congo, but I discouraged any participation in the Inga-Katanga power line. I considered it a complete waste of money. There was ample potential for small hydro dams near the copper mines in Katanga that could provide the necessary power. The thousand-mile transmission line was also designed so that power would not be available to any of the cities through which it passed, constituting a political liability.

With Nixon's blessing and lots of loan guarantees available, all of Mobutu's projects were financed, including the Inga Dam and the power line. The US Export-Import Bank provided a loan guarantee to the US company Morrison-Knudsen to build the power line. Lockheed received a loan guarantee from the US Defense Department for four C-130 military cargo aircraft. EXIM also financed airplane purchases from Boeing and McDonald Douglas.

Mobutu's state visit was not without its amusing aspects. I was too junior to be invited to the White House state dinner. But my wife, Suzanne, and I were invited to come for post-dinner coffee and dancing. We donned formal clothing and arrived at the White House around 8:30 p.m. Most of the guests had left their tables and were taking their coffee standing up. But President and Mrs. Nixon and President and Mrs. Mobutu had formed a receiving line to greet the late-coming guests, including us. When the Mobutu couple saw us approaching, they jumped out of the line and gave us both hugs with lots of greetings in French. We were old friends from the US Embassy. Nixon looked at us suspiciously, but First Lady Pat Nixon graciously took us by the hand and introduced us to some of the dignitaries. She understood that we felt just as "foreign" there as the guests of honor did. It was our first of many White House experiences.

In those days, a full state visit included three nights in Washington, and four days touring different regions of the United States in an Air Force VIP passenger aircraft. Mobutu decided that he wanted to go to Disney World in Florida. He had an entourage of about thirty countrymen. At the end of his first day in Disney World, Mobutu called me and said that he could not get over his delight at Disney's "ride" down the Congo River, with electronic crocodiles and all sorts of African phenomena. He wanted the whole family to see it. He asked me to arrange for Pan American Airways to provide a charter aircraft, at his expense, to bring over about another thirty people. That was my first experience as a diplomatic travel agent.

Nixon's refusal to allow Mobutu to purchase the F-4 fighter jet was the first of a growing number of irritations between our two governments. The Congress was becoming increasingly unhappy at the sale of sophisticated weapons systems to countries that were too underdeveloped to make use of them and who were also receiving US development assistance. For the Lockheed C-130 aircraft, I prepared a long justification that had to be submitted to the foreign affairs committees of both houses before the sale could go through. This sale was approved, but the F-4s were totally out of the question.

President Nixon did not want to be totally negative about Mobutu's air force. So, he asked the Defense Department to recommend an alternative to the F-4. DOD came up with an earlier model fighter jet that was no longer in use but could be taken out of storage. It was the Navy A-6, and Mobutu could have a flock of them just for the cost of taking them out of moth balls, about $50,000 each. It was clearly adequate for the country's needs and could be operated at low cost without the requirement for sophisticated pilot training.

Mobutu's response to the offer of the A-6 fighters was the first indication that power and fame had started to go to his head. We were accustomed to his taking our advice more or less without question. He knew that he had our support and dealt with us accordingly. But something snapped with the F-4 decision. He became incensed. He said that we were treating the Congo as a second-rate power instead of one of Africa's most important countries. Our offer of the obsolete A-6, secondhand junk, was an insult. He turned us down in a huff. It did not harm our relations, but Mobutu was sending a signal that he was a big guy now, and he wanted more respect.

In standing up to the United States, Mobutu had a backup plan. In France, General de Gaulle had come to power in 1958. In foreign policy, de Gaulle wanted to consolidate the French- speaking countries into something like the British Commonwealth, with policy coordination revolving around Paris. In view of its size and francophone population, the Congo became one of France's principal targets for incorporation into the French orbit. During my tour at the US Embassy in Kinshasa in 1966–1969, the USAID mission director told me that French embassy personnel were seeking out American contract personnel and Peace Corps volunteers, asking them questions about US government activities. The French intelligence station chief was one of my social friends. Over drinks one evening, I told him that we had no secrets about what we were doing in the Congo. He could ask us all the questions he wanted and we would answer them. There was room for everybody from the good side of the Iron Curtain.

The French paid special attention to Mobutu commensurate with the size and importance of Zaire, inviting him to Paris and sending him high-level delegations. He loved the attention. For the francophone world, Zaire had the second biggest population of French speakers. When de Gaulle resigned in early 1969, the French held a presidential election. The two candidates were Georges Pompidou for the Gaullists and François Mitterrand for the Socialists. The morning after the election, I brought visiting Assistant Secretary of State Joseph Palmer to have breakfast at Mobutu's villa. The first course was whiskey, straight. Mobutu's ear was glued to a portable shortwave radio. In the middle of breakfast, Mobutu burst into a smile. Pompidou had been elected. The Gaullists were his guys.

When Mobutu complained that the Americans had denied him state-of-the-art fighter jets, the French came to his rescue. They offered him the top French jet fighter, the Mirage, at a cost of $1.5 million each. He purchased eight. Five years later, none of them were flyable. But Mobutu had the prestige of owning them. By contrast, the American C-130 cargo planes were a success. Mobutu had four of them, and he used them effectively in moving military personnel around the Congo to put out fires, most of which entailed the suppression of political dissent. In those days, political repression had not yet started to bother us.

The silliest project coming out of Mobutu's state visit was the coast guard cutter for Lake Tanganyika, about a thousand miles east of the Congo's capital city. The cutter had to be cut into sections in order to traverse the many underpasses and other obstacles between the Atlantic port of Matadi and the eastern lake. Despite the problems, it was successfully transported to the port of Kalemie on the lake's western shore. For lack of maintenance and training, however, the ship was never really operational.

During the first half of the 1970s, Mobutu became increasingly authoritarian and intolerant of criticism. He financed three daily newspapers and disallowed any others. There were no nongovernmental voices on television or the domestic radio system. Only one political party was allowed, a practice common to virtually all of the independent African nations at the time. Mobutu's secret police kept close watch on dissidents.

As director for Central African Affairs in the State Department during 1970–1974, I did not pay too much attention to the repressive political system. The human rights issue did not become important in our Africa policy until a few years later through congressional pressure. But I did become personally involved in a serious issue between Mobutu and the Roman Catholic Archbishop of Kinshasa, Cardinal Malula, in 1973.

We received a cry for help from the Vatican through our mission to the Holy See in Rome. They said that there was heavy tension between Mobutu and the archbishop. They expressed the view that the United States government had the most influence on Mobutu and asked for our assistance. So, I was assigned to troubleshoot. My first stop was Rome, and the beautiful rooms of the Vatican foreign ministry, especially the several paintings by Raphael. I apologized to the Vatican diplomats for my lack of Italian language capability. They immediately put me at ease by insisting that their language of diplomacy was French, as it should be.

What was the problem? Malula had decided that the corruption in the Mobutu regime had become intolerable. He could no longer remain silent. He had started to include denunciations of Mobutu and the regime in his Sunday homilies. Needless to say, Mobutu was not happy about it and began making menacing threats. My response to the Vatican office in charge of diplomacy in Africa was to suggest that Malula be called to Rome for a lengthy period of consultations and cooling off. They had already suggested that to Malula, who turned it down because he feared that Mobutu would not let him come back to Zaire.

My next stop was Kinshasa and a meeting with Mobutu. We were able to speak frankly. He considered me family. I asked him what was going on with the archbishop? After all, Mobutu and his family were devout Catholics. They went to mass every Sunday. Mobutu said they had stopped going to mass when Malula started his weekly insults. He then launched into a tirade against Malula. He called him a hypocrite. "I have a list of Malula's mistresses and all of his illegitimate children. Who is he to criticize me? He is also diverting church funds to his family. He should shut up."

I told Mobutu that the Vatican was willing to call Malula to Rome for lengthy consultations if Mobutu could promise both Washington and Rome that he would allow Malula to return. Mobutu said he could accept that solution, provided that Malula understood he could not resume his public criticism after his return. That scenario was followed, and it worked out. Malula returned after one year and refrained from public criticism of Mobutu.

That was my first of many efforts at conflict resolution in Africa. What I found amusing after this incident was Mobutu's attendance at the annual mass honoring the memory of the country's first prime minister and national hero, Patrice Lumumba. There he was on his knees every year in the cathedral honoring the man he helped assassinate in 1961.

In 1973, Mobutu came to the annual meeting of the United Nations General Assembly in New York. The UN General Debate every September brings around thirty heads of state to address the UNGA for about thirty minutes each. During that week, the American secretary of state spends an entire week in New York for meetings with heads of state and foreign ministers. The American president makes a speech every year and spends a day or two in New York for important meetings.

That year, Secretary of State Henry Kissinger agreed to meet with Mobutu. As director for Central African affairs, I was assigned to be the note taker for the conversation that took place in Mobutu's suite at the Waldorf Astoria Hotel. Mobutu started with an attack on US policy toward the Portuguese refusal to give independence to their Angola colony, right next door to Zaire. He said that Portugal itself was a poor developing nation. It had no right to colonize an African nation. The United States needed to put more pressure on Portugal. In the middle of his tirade, Mobutu pointed to me and said: "There is no need to go on, I have already explained all of this to Mr. Cohen." Kissinger looked at me suspiciously. We had not met before. On issue after issue, Mobutu began the discussion and interrupted himself to say that he had already given Mr. Cohen his views.

At the end of the meeting, Kissinger said: "Mr. President, you are our best friend in Africa. I want to assure you that we will not make any major decisions in our African policy without first consulting you." We then walked out into the hall. On our way to the elevator, Kissinger turned toward me and said: "God will punish me for all those lies that I tell."

I transferred out of the Bureau of African Affairs, after thirteen years of Africa duty, in the field and in Washington, in the spring of 1974. I was sent to Paris for a required "out of area" assignment. During my three years in Paris, all of the good economic reforms sponsored by the IMF and World Bank in Zaire fell apart, and Mobutu's long slow decline began.

The problem was a sharp drop in worldwide commodity indexes. Until the mid-1970s, most of Africa was enjoying high prices for both mineral and agricultural exports. The high copper price of $1.40 per pound was keeping both the Zairian and Zambian economies in high gear. The bubble burst during 1974–1975. Other continents were bringing their products onto world exchanges, especially Brazil in Latin America and Malaysia and Indonesia in Southeast Asia. Prices dropped precipitously. Within a few months, the price of copper dropped from $1.40 to $0.75 per pound. Zaire's exports of coffee, palm oil, and maize also took a big price hit.

With his state revenue cut in half, Mobutu found himself in a corner. Most of the country's earnings had to go for debt service and the rent-seeking system. There was nothing left for maintenance and essential services such as education, health, and infrastructure. Mobutu's popularity went negative rapidly. He tried to recover by instituting a policy of "Zairianisation." All foreign-owned businesses were required to take on Zairian partners for at least 50 percent ownership. The new partners were selected for their political connections, not for their business talents. Needless to say, the economy took further hits, as many businesses were looted and ceased to exist.

In addition to the country's economic woes, Zaire's relations with neighboring countries deteriorated. Oil-rich Angola achieved independence from Portugal without preparation in 1974. A civil war among insurgent groups who had been fighting Portugal started fighting each other for power. Mobutu helped the FNLA group under Holden Roberto, who had been an insurgent operating out of Zaire. Holden's group lost the Angolan civil war to the Marxist MPLA after Cuban troops arrived to make sure that the MPLA was installed in power. Because of his support for a rival insurgent group, the Angolan government treated Mobutu with suspicion for a number of years.

Between 1974 and 1980, during a tour of duty in Paris and as ambassador to Senegal from 1977 to 1980, I had only one encounter with the Mobutu problem. In 1978, a group of Zairian insurgents invaded Katanga province from Angola and were threatening to take over the strategic copper-producing areas. I was awakened by a telephone call from the State Department operations center at 1 a.m. and informed that three US Air Force transport planes would be bringing a contingent of French and Moroccan troops to Zaire to support Mobutu's efforts to deal with the armed insurgents who had invaded from Angola. I was asked to request authorization for the aircraft to land and refuel at Dakar international airport. At the time, it was the only airport in West Africa that had fuel, water, and food available 24/7.

I asked the caller when the aircraft were due to arrive. He said 5 a.m., only four hours later. The aircraft were already airborne. I called and awakened the Senegalese prime minister with a request that he authorize the landings. He asked about the purpose of the military mission. I said that the United States, France, and Morocco were working together in order to help Mobutu fight insurgents. The prime minister instantly said that Senegal was ready to do whatever it could to help Mobutu and would also send troops. That sentiment was later repeated in Côte d'Ivoire, which also offered to send troops. That experience struck me as significant, because, for all of his antics and mismanagement, the francophone governments all felt a sense of solidarity toward Mobutu. He was clearly not a pariah in the francophone world. The insurgency was successfully defeated. The bad news was that Mobutu's ragtag army once again demonstrated its total incompetence.

In 1989, when President George H. W. Bush elevated me to the position of assistant secretary of state for Africa, I had not had any substantive contact with Mobutu for fifteen years. Certainly, I was a regular guest at the Zaire Embassy in Washington, where I had access to all the gossip. But I had had no contact with the big man. In 1989, I knew that I would be seeing Mobutu often. After twenty-six years in power, he remained the same, but his country had deteriorated beyond recognition. It was clearly a basket case.

Nevertheless, we needed Mobutu. In neighboring Angola, we were supporting an insurgency against the Marxist regime that was being kept in power by 20,000 Cuban troops. We needed Mobutu's support to use Zaire's airfields for the transit of supplies to the insurgents, known as UNITA. We also continued to count on Mobutu's support for our interests in the United Nations.

During my first visit to Kinshasa in 1989, to make sure our access to Zairian facilities was still intact and to talk with Angolan insurgent leader Jonas Savimbi, Mobutu invited me to have dinner on his official riverboat, the *Kamanyola*. During drinks before dinner, Mobutu was quite animated. He boasted about a fresh shipment of pink champagne from France, as the butler was popping the first cork. Before Mobutu could pour a glass for me, I tried to decline, as I have an allergy to that type of champagne. I said, "Maréchal, I would prefer a Coca-Cola." He couldn't believe it and continued to insist that I have his version of bubbly. After five animated exchanges, he finally relented and said to the butler in French: "Bring Minister Cohen a Coca-Cola." He then turned to me and said in heavily accented English: "I do not wish to violate your human rights."

In August 1989, Mobutu decided that the war in Angola had gone on long enough. He decided to sponsor a peace conference to bring together President Dos Santos and UNITA leader Savimbi, in the presence of as many African heads of state as he could recruit. Eighteen heads of state showed up. The conferees persuaded Dos Santos to offer Savimbi and his lieutenants full participation in the government as vice president and as ministers, with the right to run for election as an independent party. The two leaders agreed and signed the document. A few weeks later, Savimbi reneged. He told me during a private meeting in Rabat, Morocco, that he had fought too long against the Marxist regime to end up as a partner in the Marxist regime. He was fighting for a free and fair democratic election and was not yet ready to give up. In other words, he was going back to his hideout in Angola to continue the war.

Needless to say, Mobutu was outraged by Savimbi's behavior. Savimbi had signed the agreement in front of all those heads of state and then reversed course. Mobutu was embarrassed. He decided to deny access to the United States for the supply of arms and other supplies to UNITA forces in Angola. As a result, the Angolan army, with the help of Soviet advisors and Cuban logistical support, started to crush the UNITA insurgents, who retreated further and further into the southeast corner of Angola, along the Namibian border. In Washington we became quite alarmed.

We recommended that President Bush invite Mobutu to Washington for a heart-to-heart talk. During their meeting in the Oval Office, Bush asked Mobutu to reconsider, arguing that we had worked together on the Angolan project for too long to give up just when it looked as if real negotiations could take place. Mobutu said that he could not refuse a request from his good friend President Bush. He said he would immediately reopen the supply routes. In addition, he said that he would be celebrating his sixtieth birthday at his villa at Cape Martin in southern France in a few weeks. He would invite Jonas Savimbi to participate and reconcile with him at that time. He asked that Mr. Cohen also attend in order to be a witness to the reconciliation.

Mobutu's Italian-style villa at Cap Martin overlooked the Bay of Villefranche, with the city of Nice in the background. The bay was a frequent host to US naval ships. That October Sunday there was a US naval frigate sitting in the bay below the villa. As we sat around a table for drinks and reconciliation talks, Mobutu was clearly nervous about the ship's presence. At one point, he ordered staff to bring a screen to make us invisible to the ship. He said, "Those American ships have listening devices. I want this meeting to be confidential."

After reconciliation, we had the birthday lunch around the swimming pool. Mobutu had brought one of Kinshasa's most popular orchestras to play for the guests. I sat at Mobutu's table. During one song, Mobutu shed tears. He explained that he and his wife had decided to become engaged while listening to that song.

In May 1991, our efforts to mediate a real peace agreement between the Angolan factions had born fruit, and an eighteen-month transition to a democratic election started to unfold. In effect, we had gotten Jonas Savimbi what he was fighting for. As a result, our interest in Mobutu switched from support for insurgency to pressure for political and economic reform. Earlier in March 1990, Secretary of State James Baker met with Mobutu on the margins of the Namibia independence ceremonies. Baker told Mobutu that it was imperative for him to start a process of transition to multiparty democracy. If he did not do that, he would be swept away by the forces for change.

Mobutu followed Baker's advice, but he did it in his own way. He opened the political process by allowing independent media and independent political parties. That was fine. But he also spent large sums of government money creating many new "independent" parties. He wanted to dilute the political scene with many participants so that his own party, the Popular Movement for the Revolution, would continue to dominate.

Mobutu spent so much money on this effort that he had to squeeze all the money out of the state mining company, Gécamines. As a result, the copper mines were not maintained, more and more shafts became flooded, and copper exports declined from 400,000 tons per year to 50,000 tons. Already in dire straits, the economy went virtually bankrupt by mid-1992. The World Bank decided to stop providing support, and we did not object, reflecting our reduced need for Mobutu's support.

At that time, Mobutu started spending more and more time at

his palace in Gbadolite, the town of his birth near the border of the Central African Republic in the Equateur Province, about 800 miles north of Kinshasa. He clearly had given up on day-to-day governance, allowing his ministers to steal whatever was left. There were also reliable reports that he had sunk into complete decadence, requiring the services of a new fourteen-year-old virgin from the local village every day.

The last time I saw Mobutu before his downfall in 1996 was in 1994 during a visit on behalf of the Global Coalition for Africa, my second career home after retirement from the Foreign Service. As I greeted him, he turned to his entourage and said, "This is Minister Cohen. I knew him as a junior diplomat in Kinshasa twenty-eight years ago. And I knew his wife also." Shortly after that visit, I recalled a private conversation we had had in 1969 when I was chargé d'affaires at the American Embassy in Kinshasa. At that time he had said, "There is no point in trying to improve the lives of the Congolese people. They are all lazy, ungrateful cheaters."

I heard Mobutu's sentiments from other African leaders, but in more subtle terms. African people are children. They need fatherly guidance. Mobutu believed African culture requires a paramount chief to guide the people. He was the Congo's paramount chief. He provided guidance, but unfortunately he did not lead his people to economic development.

Although the majority of his people were happy to see him finally go, Mobutu left a legacy that continues to be significant today, two decades later. The Congo was stable during Mobutu's long tenure. He ruled with a strong hand. Since his departure, the Congo has been chronically unstable, especially in the eastern provinces of South Kivu, North Kivu, and Ituri. Rebel militias sponsored by neighboring Uganda and Rwanda continued to ravage these provinces in 2015, despite efforts by the international community at conflict resolution.

The Congolese government of Joseph Kabila has been incapable of restoring order. The population generally detests him. Yet, in the face of external aggression, the Congolese people are patriotic and proud of being citizens of the Congo. This general patriotic sentiment did not exist when the country became independent and tribalism and ethnic animosities were rampant. Under Mobutu's long rule, Congolese nationalism and feeling of national solidary developed. This was Mobutu's one and only legacy, but it has been important in keeping the country together against a variety of external aggressions.

The late Laurent Kabila, president of the Democratic Republic of the Congo from 1996 to 2001, at a summit conference of the African Union in Addis Ababa in 2000.
Credit: UTube.com

CHAPTER 8

Laurent-Désiré Kabila—
Democratic Republic of the Congo

The Man Who Ousted
the Despised Mobutu

Historical Note

In 1960, at the time of the independence of the Belgian Congo, Laurent Kabila was one of the few Congolese with a university degree. He studied in various institutions in Europe and received his degree from the University of Dar Es Salaam in Tanzania. He entered politics immediately after independence in his home province of Katanga, the mining center in the Congo's southeast. He supported Patrice Lumumba, the Congo's first elected prime minister. After Lumumba's assassination, he continued to use his position as a provincial legislator to support radical anti-Western positions pursuant to Lumumba's teachings.

When General Mobutu took power in a military coup in 1965, Kabila had no choice but to flee the Congo. He established himself in Kigoma, Tanzania, across Lake Tanganyika from the Congo. He started anti-Mobutu rebel operations designed to destabilize the Mobutu regime. In order to support himself, he engaged in a variety of business operations, including a restaurant, smuggling gold and timber, and, according to some reports, operating a brothel.

Kabila's rebel operations did not amount to much. Nevertheless, his big chance came in 1996, when Rwandan and Ugandan military forces invaded Zaire to clear out refugee camps harboring criminals who had perpetrated the Rwanda genocide of 1994. Both the Rwandan and Ugandan governments considered the operation to be an excellent opportunity to overthrow the corrupt dictatorship of President Mobutu. Needing a Congolese opposition political personality to organize and lead a newly recruited Congolese military force, the Rwandan and Ugandan regimes selected Laurent Kabila. The invasion and the long march across one thousand miles of Congolese territory were successful, resulting in Laurent Kabila's installation on May 17, 1997, as president of the now renamed Democratic Republic of the Congo.

In addition to his armed support from Rwanda and Uganda, Kabila received valuable military assistance from the government of Angola as he advanced through the western part of Zaire toward the capital Kinshasa. Because Mobutu was so despised both inside the Congo and internationally, the Rwandan and Ugandan invasions were considered humanitarian acts rather than aggression. There was absolutely no criticism from the international community. The Zairean population was also delighted with Mobutu's overthrow.

Kabila's rule was tumultuous and cruel. He did not hesitate to order assassinations of political enemies and those he considered to have betrayed him. He was virulently anti-Western because of the support the West had given Mobutu for four decades. He rebuffed efforts by the United States to develop close and friendly relations.

Kabila was also troubled by the close support he was receiving from the Rwandan government. His military commander was from the Rwandan Army. Rwandan intelligence agencies exercised considerable influence on politics in the capital city Kinshasa. Within months of Kabila's seizing power, the Congolese population began to see him as being under the control of the Rwandan and Ugandan governments. He decided that he needed do something drastic. In 1998, therefore, he issued a public order to the Ugandan and Rwandan governments to remove their military forces from the Congo. The two governments complied. But within a few months, they invaded the Congo once again with a new surrogate force of anti-Kabila Congolese politicians.

Kabila invoked the mutual assistance agreements of the Southern African Development Community (SADC), bringing in military forces from Angola, Zimbabwe, and Botswana. The Rwandan and Ugandan armies had to give up their bridgeheads near the capital city Kinshasa but were able to maintain control of one-third of the Congo in the mineral-rich eastern provinces. The war ended in stalemate in 2002, but Kabila was not around to witness it, because his personal bodyguard had assassinated him in January 2001. His son Joseph Kabila became president by appointment of the SADC powers, and remained the elected president as of early 2015.

The entire period after Mobutu's ouster in 1997 to late 2014 has seen poor governance, serious corruption, and grave instability in the eastern provinces because of Rwanda's and Uganda's support of rebels and militias. These two countries engaged in acts of destabilization to maintain their access to valuable minerals that had been under their control since the initial invasion of 1996.

Fifteen years after Mobutu's overthrow, many Congolese are saying that although his rule was corrupt and dictatorial, he had at least maintained stability. Since his departure, millions of Congolese have died of famine, malnutrition, and killing because of instability and war in the eastern provinces that neither Kabila regimes could bring under control.

When Laurent Kabila became president of Zaire in May 1997, one of his first acts was to change the name of the country from Zaire back to the Democratic Republic of the Congo, its original post-independence name.

Based on his less than stellar track record as an anti-Mobutu insurgent and guerrilla leader, Kabila was viewed by the international community as something of a country bumpkin when he took power. Unlike the notorious and feared Pierre Mulele, who started a significant insurgency against Mobutu from his home province of Bandundu in Central Congo, Kabila was unable to make much of an impact on the Congolese people. Even the famous Cuban revolutionary Che Guevara, who came to western Tanzania in 1965 to assist the Congolese insurgents, found Kabila to be lazy and ineffective as a guerrilla leader.

During Kabila's first few months as president, it had become clear that the real power in Kinshasa was in the hands of his Rwandan mentors. The Congolese army chief of staff, James Kaberebe, was a Rwandan general. Rwandan intelligence was essentially running the government from behind the scenes, although many of the Rwandan agents took pleasure in flaunting their power by brazenly confiscating apartments and automobiles.

By mid-1998, Kabila had become a laughingstock among the Congolese people. He was clearly seen as a stooge of the Rwandan and Ugandan regimes. He thus moved to take a bold action against the Rwandan and Ugandan forces that were effectively controlling power or risk losing all credibility with his people.

In addition to the overwhelming presence of the Rwandan and Ugandan intelligence services, Kabila was also having problems with the United States. Unlike earlier administrations that valued Mobutu as a loyal friend of the United States, the Clinton administration detested Mobutu. After Kabila's victory and the departure of Mobutu, the Africa policy makers in the Clinton administration wanted to develop close and friendly relations with Kabila, but the old guerrilla fighter would have none of it.

Kabila's message to the Clinton administration was simple. He said that he could not countenance a close relationship with a United States government that had supported his archenemy Mobutu for thirty-two years. Washington wanted to love Kabila, but Kabila did not love Washington back. Consequently, when Kabila broke with his former benefactors, Rwanda and Uganda, Washington was not too concerned about his subsequent troubles.

In July 1998, Kabila publicly ordered the governments of Rwanda and Uganda to remove all of their military forces from the Congo. Both governments complied immediately, but that was not the end of the story. They had placed Kabila in power after eight months of bloody combat against Mobutu's army, and they were not going to give up the spoils of war so easily.

Both governments immediately began recruiting anti-Kabila Congolese citizens to form a new political party and insurgent force. During August 1998, the Rwandan and Ugandan armies once again invaded the Congo, this time with the intention of ousting Kabila and installing other Congolese political surrogates who would be more grateful to their mentors.

The invasion began with a bold tactical move. The Ugandan and Rwandan commanders arranged to hijack a civilian passenger aircraft in the eastern Congolese city of Goma. They forced the crew to fly 150 commandos to the Congolese military base at Kitona, about 100 miles west of the capital city Kinshasa. With the help of anti-Kabila Congolese troops, they captured the base and began moving rapidly eastward toward Kinshasa. They aimed to overthrow Kabila as quickly as possible and thereby avoid a long land march of one thousand miles from the Congo's eastern border.

The surprise air bridge to Kitona was a brilliant maneuver, but the Ugandans and Rwandans failed to inform and consult with the government of Angola, whose northern border is only about fifty miles from the area of military activity and Kinshasa. The Angolans, who had facilitated the first invasion from the east in 1996, were not amused. Also, their intelligence had learned that the Rwandan army had been cooperating with the Angolan rebel leader Jonas Savimbi in both the smuggling of diamonds from Angola and the movement of arms into Angola for use against the Angolan army. Hence, the Angolans did not like the idea of Rwandan forces operating so close to their northern border where Savimbi's guerrillas could receive assistance for their operations inside Angola.

The Angolan military deployed their air force against the Rwandan and Ugandan troops as they moved eastward toward Kinshasa. Also, invoking the mutual assistance treaty of the Southern African Development Community, Kabila asked for military assistance to fight the invaders. Zimbabwe and Botswana sent their military units in response. The result was that the Rwandan and Ugandan commandos were forced to abandon their march toward Kinshasa and were able to avoid being trapped only by moving through the forests of northern Angola under the guidance of Savimbi's UNITA guerrillas.

While Kabila was able to remain in power in Kinshasa with the help of Angola, Zimbabwe, and Botswana, his troubles were just beginning. Unopposed in the eastern Congo, the Rwandan and Ugandan armies were easily able to conquer and occupy a full 40 percent of the Congo's territory, and were quite prepared to begin exploiting the eastern region's vast mineral resources. The arrival of Zimbabwean troops helped stop the invaders from moving beyond their occupied zone toward the western Congo, but a long and costly stalemated war went on until an international mediation brought a cease-fire and peace agreement in 2002. During this four-year period, millions of civilian Congolese in the occupied territories died of malnutrition, disease, and war-related killing. The conflict was called "Africa's first world war."

I observed the first six months of the war in the Congo from my office at the Global Coalition for Africa. I found the absence of any reaction from the United States and the general international community quite incredible. The governments of Rwanda and Uganda were committing naked aggression against a sovereign government, and Washington was saying nothing. I had read about the revenge of spurned lovers in novels, but Washington's reaction to Kabila's refusal to accept Washington's embrace was bizarre to say the least. The Clinton administration accepted without question the dubious claims of Rwanda and Uganda that they had to send in their forces in order to thwart their own dissidents, who were mounting cross-border guerrilla operations against them from Congolese territory.

In early 1999, after I had resigned from the Global Coalition for Africa, I received a call from a Congolese friend who was also close to the Kabila family, which shared the same ethnic group in northern Katanga province. My friend told me that Kabila might be willing to normalize relations with Washington and asked me if I would be available to advise Kabila about this. I accepted in principle and went to Kinshasa to meet with Kabila.

I was a bit surprised that Kabila would be willing to consult me. During the period 1966 to 1969, when I was the deputy ambassador, I became close to Mobutu and was responsible for deploying US, Turkish, and other military assets against Kabila and other anti-Mobutu fighters.

My first reaction to Kabila was one of amusement. He was sitting at an elevated desk that made it seem as if he were in the mezzanine and I was looking up from the ground floor. He was friendly. I did not find the country bumpkin that I envisaged. He had plenty of smarts. His vision for the Congo was aimed at uplifting the rural farmers and the urban poor. Who could argue with that? He was basking in the admiration of the Congolese people, who totally supported his ultimatum to the Rwandan and Ugandan governments.

I could not discern from our conversations that he had begun to eliminate Congolese enemies through extrajudicial assassinations.

He was also busy recruiting Rwandan and Ugandan exile fighters to help him fight those governments in the east. He was thereby justifying the accusations that he was harboring and arming former perpetrators of genocide in Rwanda.

Out in the streets of Kinshasa, I found a lot less tension than I had seen over many years under Mobutu. The Rwandan and Ugandan attack had mobilized the Congolese people against the aggressors and in support of Kabila. There was also a nasty ethnic element. The significant population of Congolese Tutsis had come under suspicion of supporting the Tutsi rulers of Rwanda and became the subject of discrimination and violence. Thousands had to flee to Rwanda as refugees. Kabila's propagandists were fueling this fire in the media.

Kabila agreed to retain my consulting firm, Cohen and Woods, to lobby for him in Washington. Payment was sporadic and usually in cash taken out of a shoebox. My first piece of advice was to revive a UN Security Council Resolution aimed at investigating mass murder in the Congolese village of Tingi Tingi in 1996.

After they had broken up their refugee camps on the Congo side of the border, Rwandan troops advanced westward from the border in pursuit of Rwandan exiles refusing to return to Rwanda. They concluded that Hutu refugees that refused to return to Rwanda were by definition perpetrators of genocide. Allegedly, the Rwandan troops caught up with the fleeing refugees at Tingi Tingi, near the regional capital Kisangani. According to eyewitness reports, the Rwandan Hutus were separated from Congolese villagers and summarily executed.

Kabila had not allowed the UN investigators to move around beyond the capital city, so the investigation was postponed. I recommended to Kabila that the investigation be resumed, because his former Rwandan allies might well be blamed for genocide. There were lots of witnesses around to tell the story. He agreed. However, when I spoke to UN officials two years after the alleged atrocities, I heard, "Let sleeping dogs lie." They had their hands full trying to manage new major conflict in the eastern Congo and did not want to start an argument over stale allegations against Rwanda, one of the major protagonists in the new war.

The State Department's Bureau of African Affairs was quite

disillusioned with Kabila because of his initial hostility and did not respond kindly to my entreaties to help Kabila repel the aggressions of Uganda and Rwanda. On the contrary, in the State Department's view, there was no question of aggression on the part of Rwanda and Uganda. It was a civil war, plain and simple, and the State Department had moved into a conflict resolution mode.

The protagonists in the Congolese civil war were the Kabila regime on the one hand, and the new Congolese armed opposition party, the Congrès National pour la Démocratie (CND) that was receiving "support" from "foreign" governments. Rwanda and Uganda were in the Congo to exercise their self-defense right to combat guerrillas working to destabilize them from bases inside the Congolese border. CND leaders received visas allowing them to visit the United States to inform everyone that they wanted to oust Kabila in order to establish real democracy. Kabila was just a clone of Mobutu, according to them. None of the Congolese citizens living in the Washington area that I knew were convinced. They were all on Kabila's side.

While the State Department's Bureau of African Affairs could not abide anti-Rwanda and anti-Uganda arguments, there was one high American government official who had an open mind. He was the late ambassador Richard Holbrooke, United States Permanent Representative to the United Nations during 1998 to 2001. Holbrooke had succeeded earlier in a triumphal negotiation to bring about peace in the Balkans among Serbia, Croatia, and Bosnia through the historic Dayton Accords.

I told Holbrooke that President Kabila, having ousted the hated Mobutu, did not deserve to be so disrespected by the American government. Holbrooke understood. During a period when he held the chair as president of the UN Security Council in the year 1999, Holbrooke took some initiatives that temporarily but effectively grabbed Africa policy away from the State Department and transferred it to his office in New York.

One of his initiatives was to call a summit conference in New York of all the heads of state involved in the war in the Congo as of late 1999. He particularly wanted to bring Kabila together with Rwandan president Paul Kagame and Ugandan president Yoweri Museveni. He thought he might be able to repeat his success in the

Balkans by bringing about a negotiated peace in the Congo. As far as I could tell, Holbrooke did all of this without any consultation with the Bureau of African Affairs, the White House, or any other US government entity.

Holbrooke sent out the invitations in his capacity as president of the UN Security Council. To my chagrin, everyone accepted except President Laurent Kabila. I asked my Congolese friends to set up a phone call with Kabila. We spoke at length about the invitation. Kabila told me that he did not want to set foot in the country that had supported Mobutu for thirty-two years. He hated the United States, and the United States hated him.

I assured Kabila that technically he would not be visiting the United States. He would be coming to international territory within New York City. He would not be coming to Washington or any other area of the United States. When I informed him that he would receive full protection as a head of state from the United States Secret Service, he really became upset. After all, his equivalent of the secret service was his arm for assassinating his enemies in the Congo.

After two long conversations, along with parallel support from our mutual Congolese friends, Kabila agreed to come to New York. When I saw Kabila in New York shortly after his arrival, he said to me, "I am here only because of you. If anything goes wrong, it will be your fault."

After a few hours together in the Security Council's meeting room, Kabila, Kagame, and Museveni shook hands and agreed to work toward a peaceful solution. That was the real beginning of the peace process in the eastern Congo, but it was only after the George W. Bush administration came into office in January 2001 that the US government became stern with the Rwandan and Ugandan heads of state. Secretary of State Colin Powell told Rwandan president Kagame in 2001 to take his troops out of the Congo, and he complied.

What struck me most about Kabila's visit to New York was his popularity with the Congolese diaspora community. They flocked to his hotel to pay tribute. He had done two things to make them proud. First, he had ousted Mobutu. By 1996, Mobutu had lost all support within the Congolese population. Secondly, he had stood up against Rwanda and Uganda, which were pillaging their country's resources.

Kabila's anti-Tutsi propaganda that had put a whole ethnic group in danger did not seem to bother anyone except the Tutsis themselves. They were depicted as betraying the Congo in favor of their ethnic kin in Rwanda. It was xenophobia at its worst. Neither did Kabila's fascistic actions against his domestic enemies bother any of the Congolese.

It was at this point that I decided to stop working for Kabila, because I had done all I could. He had succeeded in establishing international legitimacy through his UN performance, and from that point he was welcome in a succession of African summits as a full equal. I did see him one more time in 2000 in Sirte, Libya, where I asked him to liberate a young American missionary who had been arrested in Kinshasa for inadvertently photographing the headquarters of Congo intelligence. He did that without hesitation, indicating that while he hated the United States government, he did not necessarily hate the American people.

On January 18, 2001, Kabila was assassinated by one of his security guards. There were many people interested in his demise. While some persons in his immediate entourage were executed for the crime, the paymaster has never been identified.

Kabila's thirty-year-old son Joseph Kabila took over as interim president until peace could be established through negotiations. After a cease-fire in 2002, South Africa provided mediation services that led to an interim government of national unity, followed by full elections in 2006. Joseph Kabila was elected and was re-elected in 2012.

Unfortunately, the peace process and the elections did not lead to real peace in the eastern Congo. While Rwandan and Ugandan troops had left as of 2001, both countries continued to sponsor armed militias that guaranteed their continued access to resources that they had been controlling for over six years as occupiers. Peace or no peace, they would not give up that lucrative source of revenue. As of early 2015, the people of the eastern Congo were still suffering from war, hunger, and disease. Like his father, Joseph Kabila has been unable to deal with the vital issues. The international community continues to grope for solutions.

GROUP IV

The Military Chiefs:
Soldiers Do Not Do Democracy

The former military ruler of the Federal Republic of Nigeria, General Ibrahim Babangida (center) greets visitors to his retirement home in the town of Minna in central Nigeria in 2007.
Credit: Vanguard Press

CHAPTER 9

Ibrahim Babangida—Nigeria

The General Who Found
Democracy Inconvenient

Historical Note

The history of the Federal Republic of Nigeria since its independence from the United Kingdom in 1960 is essentially one of alter-
nating civilian and military rule. A destructive internal war during
the period 1967–1970 reinforced the role of the military in Nigeria's
path toward maturity as one of Africa's most important nations.
During the period 1960 to 1993, there were five military coups that
brought military commanders to power. The fourth coup, in 1985,
was the work of Major General Ibrahim Babangida, then chief of
army staff to President Muhammadu Buhari, himself an army general turned dictator.

In addition to periodic military rule, the subject of ethnic rivalry
has also been a significant element in Nigeria's political evolution
since independence. In their wisdom, the British colonialists decided to merge the southern Nigerian colonies bordering on the Atlantic Ocean with the northern colonies that are part of the Sahelian
zone, bordering on the great northern Sahara Desert. The northern
peoples are mostly Muslim, and the southern peoples are a great
mixture of ethnic groups and religions, with the majority being
Christian. The politics of Nigeria have to a great extent reflected
the ethnic and religious rivalries of its different geographic regions.

Adding to the tensions between military and civilian rulers, as
well as the rivalries between diverse ethnic and religious peoples,
has been the predominance of crude oil production in Nigeria's
economy. The role of oil revenue has greatly exacerbated the

sociopolitical dilemma of government corruption as a poison in Nigerian society.

Despite its many internal problems of poor governance and ethnic/religious rivalries for power, Nigeria remains one of Africa's most important countries, with over 170 million people, a strong military, and the largest oil production on the African continent. Nigeria has to be taken seriously when it comes to Africa's role in the world.

It was May 1986. I was working in my office in the State Department's Office of the Director General of the Foreign Service. I was the principal deputy assistant secretary. That office has since been renamed the Bureau of Human Resources.

I took a call from one of my oldest friends, Ambassador H. Donald Gelber, the chargé d'affaires at the American Embassy in Lagos, then capital of the Federal Republic of Nigeria. Don and I had been classmates at the Thomas Jefferson High School in New York City and at the City College of New York. We both decided to have careers in the US diplomatic service. While I specialized in US-Africa relations, Don specialized in the diplomacy of US military relations with countries worldwide. He played an important role in the establishment of US-Turkish military relations within NATO during the 1970s, for example.

Don called me because he had a special request from President Ibrahim Babangida, the president of Nigeria. As an expert on the military who knew how to talk to high-ranking military officers, Don had become well acquainted with General Babangida before the general led the coup to overthrow President Buhari in August 1985.

President Babangida, it seemed, was very interested in the bombing of Tripoli, Libya, by the American Air Force on April 15, 1986. President Ronald Reagan had ordered the bombing in retaliation for Libya's terrorist attack on a nightclub in West Berlin called La Belle Discotheque, a hangout for American military servicemen and women. By the time this terrorist attack had occurred, President Reagan had already become fed up with Libyan "Leader"

Muammar Gaddafi because of his support to revolutionaries in the Middle East, Northern Ireland, and the Far East.

Don asked if I could obtain release of the aerial photos of Tripoli that showed the damage done by the US air bombardment. He asked that I bring the imagery to Lagos and personally explain the data to President Babangida and his military colleagues. I warmed to that idea, because I needed a break from personnel management, and the thought of heading back to Africa for a brief period was exciting. I went to the Bureau of Intelligence and Research, where I had spent four years, from 1980 to 1984. My friends there gathered the necessary aerial photos and sent me off to Nigeria.

President Babangida, accompanied by colleagues, received Don Gelber and me around 11 p.m. in his Dodon Barracks office in Lagos. Except for Mobutu of Zaire/Congo, many military heads of state in Africa tended to receive visitors in the late hours of the night. I talked them through the photos of the damage done to Gaddafi's military camp. They enjoyed it immensely and spent a lot of time going over the details. At one point Babangida said to me, "You hit the French ambassador's house. I bet you did it on purpose because the French did not give you overflight rights for this mission."

After Babangida and his buddies finished chuckling over the damage evidence, I realized that they were pleased because of their hatred for Gaddafi. That was just about the time that Gaddafi had proclaimed that he was more African than Arab and would henceforth spend most of his time helping Africans. Babangida knew that Gaddafi would be bribing the less fortunate African leaders to pay attention to him and make him look statesmanlike. Babangida decided that Nigeria would have none of it. They were too proud, and coincidentally too rich from crude oil.

I saw Babangida again about six months later, in January 1987, after I had transferred to the National Security Council staff as President Reagan's special assistant and senior director for Africa. Secretary of State George Shultz invited me to join his delegation for official visits to several African countries, including Nigeria.

Babangida made a good impression on Shultz, who saw him as a leader with a good knowledge of the key issues facing Africa and of the importance of US-Nigerian relations. Babangida also had a good grasp of the economic issues of the day, especially the pressure the World Bank and International Monetary Fund were exerting on African countries to undertake economic reform programs in order to get out from under heavy international debt loads.

Babangida told Shultz that Nigeria was in need of a World Bank–IMF program because of its heavy debt load. More than half of Nigeria's earnings from crude oil exports were going to service debt. There was not much left to provide for necessary social services. As he did with the other African countries we visited, Shultz encouraged Babangida to follow the World Bank/IMF advice.

One subject that Shultz did not raise was democracy. The fact that Babangida had come to power via a military coup did not raise any eyebrows in Washington. Indeed, it was somewhat normal for Africa in those days. It was only in the next administration, that of President George H. W. Bush, that democracy promotion became an important element of American foreign policy worldwide. The other side of Bush's new emphasis on democracy was the beginning of severe disapproval of military coups, especially those overturning democratically elected regimes.

I next visited with Babangida in August 1990 when I was assistant secretary of state for African affairs under George H. W. Bush. In the interim, Babangida addressed the issue of a possible request to the World Bank and IMF for assistance with an economic reform program. He consulted the population on the issue by addressing the nation on television and requesting that discussions take place throughout Nigeria. He wanted to make sure that everyone understood that such a program would require considerable belt-tightening in return for international assistance in restructuring debt.

As reported in the Nigerian press, discussion groups were formed throughout the nation, especially on university campuses. The reaction of the Nigerian people was interesting. They expressed willingness to undertake the sacrifices associated with economic reform, but they rejected the offer of assistance from the international financial institutions. Their reasoning was impeccable. "The World Bank and International Monetary Fund will lend us money at favorable rates so that we can decrease our debt load. But that money will disappear into the pockets of corrupt politicians, and the Nigerian people will not see a penny of it."

Babangida decided to meet the challenge. He introduced an economic restructuring program that mirrored the one proposed by the World Bank and IMF. According to economists who followed the program, the Nigerian economy improved significantly, with a decrease in inflation and a rising standard of living, at least for urban dwellers.

My meeting with Babangida in August 1990 had a specific purpose. The Republic of Liberia, a small country in Nigeria's neighborhood, was in the midst of a destructive civil war. On Christmas Eve 1989, a band of Liberian rebels crossed the border into Liberia from neighboring Côte d'Ivoire with the objective of overthrowing the government of President Samuel Doe. These rebels, led by a former Liberian high government official named Charles Taylor, were trained in Libya and financed and supported by the governments of Côte d'Ivoire and Burkina Faso.

My instruction from the White House was to avoid taking charge of the Liberian problem and to allow regional African actors to organize conflict resolution activities. Nevertheless, there was considerable pressure on Washington to become actively involved with Liberia, coming from the large Liberian diaspora community living throughout the United States. By August 1990, the internal situation in Liberia was grave, with considerable suffering and dying among the Liberian people. Rebel leader Charles Taylor had succeeded in conquering most of Liberia, but the capital city Monrovia was holding out. The sanitary and food supply situations in Monrovia were horrible.

The White House instructed me to travel to the West African region in August 1990 to consult with leaders about the Liberian tragedy. One of my stops was in Lagos to consult with President Babangida.

I found Babangida to be watching the Liberian situation very closely. There were a large number of Nigerians living in Liberia as business and professional people. Babangida was worried about their welfare. He told me that several thousands of his people appeared to be trapped by the fighting in Monrovia, and he worried about their safety.

Babangida was also livid about the surrogate nature of the war. He was angry with Côte d'Ivoire president Houphouët-Boigny and

Burkina Faso president Blaise Compaore for their total sponsorship of Charles Taylor under the overall direction of the hated Muammar Gaddafi. He said that the West Africans had to do something about it.

Since I was following instructions not to bring the United States into the Liberian civil war as a mediator nor in any other way, I encouraged Babangida to organize an armed intervention. He told me that he was thinking of an intervention by ECOWAS, the Economic Community of West African States. I told him that was a good idea, but Côte d'Ivoire and Burkina Faso would veto the proposal as ECOWAS members in good standing. Babangida acknowledged the veto problem but said the English-speaking countries would go ahead anyway.

At a summit meeting of ECOWAS shortly after my tour of the region, Nigeria, Ghana, Sierra Leone, and the francophone Republic of Guinea proposed an armed "peacekeeping" intervention in Liberia's civil war. As expected, Côte d'Ivoire and Burkina Faso disagreed, but the proposers went ahead and formed an intervention force called ECOMOG, short for ECOWAS Monitoring Group.

ECOMOG announced that they were coming to Liberia in peace with the objective of organizing a free and fair election. Charles Taylor would be eligible to campaign and run. Unfortunately, Côte d'Ivoire, Burkina Faso, and Libya had invested too heavily in Charles Taylor to take the chance that he might run for president of Liberia and lose. As a result, Taylor did not accept the ECOMOG proposal for a cease-fire and transition to an election. He wanted more war, and with the help of his friends, he continued to fight ECOMOG until the war finally ground to a negotiated cease-fire in 1997. An election followed, with Taylor winning the presidency quite handily, but Liberia was totally destroyed.

The Liberia crisis demonstrated the thinking of Babangida and other Anglophone leaders of West Africa about the French-speaking countries. They saw leaders like Félix Houphouët-Boigny and Blaise Compaore as stooges of France. Babangida saw their action in Liberia as a surrogate war on behalf of France that allegedly wanted Liberia's vast mineral, rubber, and timber resources. The only French-speaking country on Babangida's side was the Republic of Guinea, which had a unique history of bad relations with France dating back to colonial days.

After President Bush decreed in 1989 that the United States would begin vigorously promoting democracy around the world, a movement toward multiparty democracy became active in sub-Saharan Africa. This was due only partly to the new American policy. Many university-educated African intellectuals in the younger generation began agitating for more open societies.

In Nigeria, President Babangida heard the call as well. The Nigerians were fed up with military rule. They wanted multiparty democracy. But as in the case of economic reform, Babangida wanted to bring about democratic reform his own Nigerian way. He saw the electoral chaos in other African countries, where the advent of multiparty politics led to the formation of as many as fifty parties, most of which represented individual families rather than thousands of citizens.

Babangida decided that Nigeria would be a two-party state like the United States and Great Britain. He therefore created two parties by fiat, one left of center and one right of center. The leftwing party was called the Social Democratic Party (SDP), the rightwing party the National Republican Convention (NRC).

The two parties were duly formed and held nominating conventions. In February 1993 they chose Moshood Abiola from the southwestern region as the SDP candidate, and Bashr Tofa, from northern Nigeria as the NRC candidate.

In March 1993, I had a weird experience during my final days as assistant secretary. I received a call from an old Nigerian business friend, Antonio Deinde Fernandez. He was living in New York, where he was the deputy permanent representative of Mozambique to the United Nations.

Fernandez had come to Washington for a short visit and asked me to meet him for drinks at the Fairfax Hotel near Washington's Dupont Circle. He said that he wanted me to meet some visiting Nigerians. When I arrived at the hotel, I found Fernandez with two Nigerian military officers wearing the stars of general officers.

When the conversation turned to Babangida's experiment with two-party democracy, I saw the two generals tighten up visibly. One of them said through clenched teeth, "Those two candidates are just a couple of jokers. We in the military will not allow either of them to come to power."

I was dumbfounded. What was I supposed to do with that information? I had about three weeks left on the job. I was slated to leave the Bureau of African Affairs. I was going to the Global Coalition for Africa as a senior advisor on leave from the State Department. I decided that the informal nature of the information made it impossible for me to do anything. I just kept it to myself.

The election took place in June 1993. All observers gave the independent electoral commission high marks for a truly free, fair, and transparent election. There were no complaints of fraud. The winner was Moshood Abiola of the SDP.

Shortly after the election, Babangida announced that the election had been annulled. He did not give a reason. He also announced that veteran politician Ernest Shonekan would head up an interim government to prepare a new election. Lots of people were angered by this decision, especially Abiola's many supporters. There was a certain amount of violence.

Shonekan attempted to establish his interim government, but there was yet another military coup in August 1993, with Army Chief of Staff Sani Abacha carrying out Nigeria's fifth military coup. Why Babangida annulled the election that everyone said was so well done remained a mystery. When the annulment took place, I thought of that conversation with the two Nigerian generals in March. Babangida was probably aware of the discontent within the military with the two candidates for president. Perhaps he annulled the election in order to head off a military coup but was unsuccessful.

Sani Abacha died suddenly in 1998. By this time, the military hierarchy had become tired of trying to rule Nigeria. They wanted to return this poisoned chalice to the civilians. This state of affairs resulted in a new constitution and the beginning of a new period of multiparty democracy. Elections were held in 1999, and retired General Olusegun Obasanjo was elected. He himself had taken power in a military coup in 1976, when he was an army general. He had ruled the country from 1976 to 1979, when he voluntarily returned the country to multiparty democracy. Because of his "democratic" reputation, Obasanjo was easily elected as a civilian politician in 1999. Nevertheless, Obasanjo's political influence reflected once again the great power of the military in Nigerian politics.

The last time I saw Babangida was in 2004 at his home in Minna in Niger State, about two hours' drive from the new capital Abuja. I found him living in affluent circumstances, with a home full of visitors. He was serene and full of ideas about governance in Nigeria. He clearly had not given up on the idea of returning to power as a civilian political leader. He made several attempts to move back into presidential politics, but none survived for more than a short period. Perhaps his still unexplained cancellation of Nigeria's only free and fair election since independence has remained to haunt him.

The late "Leader" of the Islamic Republic of Libya, Muammar al-Gaddafi, during a press photo opportunity at the United Nations, New York, September 23, 2000.
Credit: New York Daily News.com

CHAPTER 10

Muammar Muhammad Abu Minyar al-Gaddafi — Libya

Just Call Me "Brother Leader"

Historical Note

Libya gained its independence from Italy in 1951. The first government was a monarchy under King Idris, based in the eastern city of Benghazi.

Muammar Gaddafi was born in 1942 near the city of Sirte on the Mediterranean, halfway between Benghazi and Tripoli. In 1961, he entered the military college in Benghazi. The course included four months of training in the United Kingdom.

The decade of the 1960s was one of growing nationalism and anti-capitalist sentiments in the Arab world. The great hero of the restless younger generation was Gamal Abdel Nasser, the colonel who overthrew the feudal Egyptian monarchy. In 1969, Gaddafi and a group of his fellow younger military officers staged a bloodless coup that overthrew the Idris monarchy. They established the Revolutionary Command Council, with Gaddafi as the president and chief of state. Between 1969 and 1977, Gaddafi consolidated his power by marginalizing his initial revolutionary colleagues.

In 1977, he assumed total power. He abolished the constitution and the RCC and established the Libyan Arab Jamahiriya (loosely translated as "people's revolution"). He stepped down as head of state and assumed the title of "Brother Leader of the Revolution." Under his system, the political power was supposed to belong to revolutionary committees, building up from the villages. The committees existed, but in reality Gaddafi and his family exercised all the power and controlled all of the oil revenues. His secret police,

total censorship of the media, ruthless assassinations of real or sus-
pected opponents, and financial bribery of tribal and clan leaders
guaranteed his total power. It was this power that went to his head
and made him into a total megalomaniac.

A strong believer in Arab nationalism, Gaddafi used his oil revenue to promote revolution in other Arab countries and in African countries where Islam was predominant. He set up training
camps for African guerilla fighters and became actively involved
in civil conflicts in Chad, Sudan, Liberia, and Sierra Leone. He also
financed Islamic rebels in the Philippines and Irish Catholic IRA
fighters in Northern Ireland.

Gaddafi's operatives bombed American military personnel in
Germany and blew up a Pan American Airways flight over Lockerbie, Scotland, in 1988. These actions resulted in total UN sanctions
against Libya between 1989 and 2002. After the US military actions
against Iraq in 1991, Gaddafi decided to stop supporting revolution. He also gave up his stock of chemical weapons as well as his
embryonic efforts to develop nuclear weapons. Libya returned to
the mainstream of the international community in 2002.

The "Arab Spring" hit Libya in 2011 with an anti-Gaddafi civilian uprising in Benghazi. With no confidence in his own Libyan
military, Gaddafi deployed African mercenary troops from countries immediately to Libya's south, with orders to kill all rebels
without mercy. This brought NATO air power into the conflict, resulting in Gaddafi's defeat and his capture and death at the hands
of armed rebels in his birth city of Sirte.

It was a chilly day in December 1996. I was in Tunisia participating in an American investor delegation. Leading the delegation
was a Tunisian-Italian business entrepreneur who believed that
the American business community could benefit from more exposure to private sector opportunities in Tunisia. The Tunisian had an
American business office in Washington, D.C., managed by a friend
of mine, Steve Hayes. Steve had extensive international experience,
mainly in the nongovernmental-organization sector. He persuaded
me to join the delegation in view of my career experience on the

African continent. I had retired from the US Foreign Service in November 1993.

Toward the end of the visit, we were in southern Tunisia. Our Tunisian sponsor asked Steve Hayes and me to join him for tea. He asked if we would be interested in accompanying him across the Libyan border for a meeting with Muammar Gaddafi. We were both incredulous, but we agreed to consider it. I called the State Department to request information about economic sanctions against Libya and the rules about American travelers. They told me that travel to Libya was not forbidden, but I could not use my American passport and I could not spend any money. Our Tunisian host said that he would guarantee that our passports would not be stamped and that he would cover all expenses. So, off we went across the border in a high-speed automobile.

Steve and I were not without apprehensions. After all, UN sanctions were being enforced against Libya almost universally. Gaddafi was totally isolated. None of the other Arab states were prepared to violate UN sanctions. None showed any solidarity with Gaddafi. International air links to Libya were totally suspended. The only way to travel to Tripoli was by vehicle from Tunisia or by overnight ocean ferry from Malta. We were not sure what awaited us.

We stopped at the Libyan border post but were waived through with no examination. Three hours later we were in our hotel in Tripoli, and one hour after that we were in Gaddafi's office in the Tripoli military camp. There he was in an elegant wood-paneled library, bundled up in a heavy World War Two olive drab US enlisted man's military overcoat that went right down to his toes.

The only other Libyan present was an Arabic-English interpreter. Gaddafi spoke in Arabic but did not require a translation of our English statements.

The conversation was relaxed and somewhat rambling. But it was clear that Gaddafi was hungry for authentic information about US foreign policy. He appeared to be starved for true facts. And he also found it hard to understand what he did know. The main theme was his inability to fathom US policy toward the Middle East. "How is it possible," he asked, "for the United States to favor ten million Israelis over one hundred million Arabs? It makes absolutely no sense."

He also revealed a distinct strain of paranoia. At one point he jumped into the middle of a sentence to ask, "Why does the CIA destabilize countries all over the world?" The question had no relevance to the issue we were discussing. I must have had a surge of adrenalin, as I responded to his outburst with, "Leader, we are a superpower. That is what we do." I was lucky that he smirked.

Gaddafi's overall approach was the equivalent of "I can't figure you guys out. Do you want to reform me? Do you want to overthrow me?" His famed arrogance was not there, but he tried to project self-confidence. He was looking for answers. After President Reagan's bombing of Tripoli in 1986, and after the senior Bush administration's ability to rally worldwide sanctions against Libya, Gaddafi's view of the United States had changed from contempt to respect. Libya's sabotage of the Pan American flight over Lockerbie in 1988 had made Gaddafi and his cronies total pariahs.

That first visit to Brother Leader was followed by brainstorming sessions over several months with some of Gaddafi's close advisors, led by his ambassador in Rome. We met in our Tunisian sponsor's apartment in Milan. The driving theme was always the same. "If we do what Washington wants, will we be double-crossed? How can we be sure that the US will keep its word?" It was all centered on Gaddafi's security and image. How do we get Brother Leader back to the mainstream of the international community?

In some of our less formal sessions, Gaddafi's top advisers were quite open with us. One of them told us quite frankly that Gaddafi ordered the blowing up of the Pan American Airways flight over Lockerbie. They said that Gaddafi really had no choice. President Reagan had bombed Tripoli. Gaddafi's adopted daughter had been killed. Under Libyan tribal law, blood had to be answered with blood. That was the normal order of things.

Gaddafi also took revenge against the French, who had shot down one of his air force bombers over Chad. I remember seeing an order from the Leader to his air force to shoot down a French passenger airliner overflying Libya between Paris and any one of several African capitals. The Libyan fighter jets were unable to carry out the order because the French air company UTA flew their passenger jets much too high over Libya. The fighters could not go that high. The fallback was to put a bomb on a UTA aircraft that exploded over Chad on November 19, 1989, killing all the passengers and crew. One of the passengers was Bonnie Pugh, wife of the American ambassador to Chad.

Between December 1996 and early 2002, we met with Gaddafi five more times. Two of the meetings took place in Sirte, the coastal city closest to Gaddafi's birthplace. He was trying to build a new capital there, halfway between Tripoli and Benghazi.

At each of these meetings, almost all late at night in a tent away from any regular roads, Gaddafi demonstrated additional aspects of his quirky personality, as well as his extensive reading of the world press.

Prior to one meeting, Steve Hayes and I were waiting for a signal that the Leader was ready to receive us. I brought up the subject of breaking off diplomatic relations with governments that we greatly disapproved of, like Libya and Iran. I expressed the view that diplomacy assures communications between governments, including unpleasant communications. The absence of diplomatic relations guarantees zero communications. I cited World War Two when the OSS station chief in Berne, Switzerland, Allen Dulles, maintained a frosty liaison with his Nazi counterpart.

Several hours later, in our meeting with Gaddafi, he insisted on the importance of normalizing relations between Libya and the United States. He said that Libya needed the United States, especially its technology. He took out a map of the Libyan oil patch. He said, "The squares that are colored red are reserved for the return of American oil companies. They have the best oil and gas technology." (American oil companies were required to depart Libya in 1986 when the US Congress invoked major economic sanctions against Libya.)

"We also want American dry land agricultural technology. Mr. Cohen, the next time you come to visit, please introduce me to some American experts in dry land farming."

Gaddafi finished the discussion at a theoretical level. "Diplomatic relations should not be based on whether or not two governments like each other. Diplomatic relations should be based on the importance of communications, even with governments the US may not like. Look, even during the Second World War, the US and

Nazi Germany were communicating through agents based in neutral Switzerland." Muammar, where did you hear that?

That reminded me of an earlier visit when I got off the hotel elevator at a floor below mine by mistake. I walked to what I thought was my room, and found the door slightly ajar. When I looked inside, I saw several guys with ear buds and recording devices. I quickly withdrew.

Shortly after that meeting, I was in Tucson, Arizona, for a speaking engagement. I asked my host to introduce me to the Agriculture Department at University of Arizona. I had a good talk with the department chair and a few of his associates. I described Gaddafi's interest in dry land farming as practiced in the American southwest. The professors told me that an international agreement had guaranteed Arizona a steady supply of water from the Colorado River for irrigation. Because of that deal, dry land farming had become obsolete. The university was no longer teaching the subject. "If Gaddafi really wants to get the latest and best expertise on dry land farming, he should talk to Israel." That killed that subject as far as my relations with Gaddafi were concerned.

In the year 2000, some Libyan academics, some teaching in Europe, came up with the idea for a US-Libyan Dialogue. Discussions would be limited to nongovernmental organizations and individuals. I was among those invited from the start. With lots of funding from "unknown" sources, Libyans and Americans met in various venues, including Malta, Tunisia, and Maastricht in The Netherlands. The discussions were quite frank. I remember one US academic berating the Libyans for not offering to provide relief supplies to Turkish earthquake victims who were fellow Muslims, while they were providing arms and explosives to Muslims in the Philippines and Catholic revolutionaries in Northern Ireland. The American academics were virtually all very pro-Palestinian and anti-Israel and therefore well liked by their Libyan colleagues.

During one of these meetings in London, an American oil company representative who had been allowed to return to Libya to look at the company's properties told me that the Libyans had been maintaining the American production facilities quite competently. What impressed him was the Libyans' insistence on keeping American equipment and American systems, like 110-volt electric current.

Toward the end of the 1990s, the US-Libyan Dialogue changed into the US-UK-Libyan Dialogue. Meetings were organized and chaired by the prestigious Royal Institute of International Affairs (Chatham House) in London, under the open sponsorship of Seif al-Islam Gaddafi, one of the Leader's sons. Needless to say, the luxury level of the meetings rose considerably after he took over. We had meetings in luxury resorts in Southampton, England, and Malaga, Spain.

At the end of our two-day sessions, Seif came to the final dinners, projecting an image of the reasonable, moderate intellectual with a modernization agenda. He told us he wanted Libya to open up to the international community and join the mainstream of trading industrialized nations. We also heard that he was studying at the London School of Economics in pursuit of a PhD. With a good dose of wishful thinking, we all expressed the wish that Seif would inherit the leadership after Gaddafi departed.

After the Benghazi uprising in 2011, Seif was the main voice of the Gaddafi regime, exhorting the Libyan population to support their "Leader." As the situation deteriorated, he remained loyal. After his father's death, he tried to escape south to the Republic of Niger but was apprehended by an ethnic group hostile to his own. As of late 2014 he was awaiting trial by a Libyan court at such time as the judicial system is rebuilt.

During one meeting with Gaddafi in his sprawling office compound in Tripoli, we met in an open-atrium pedestrian space, in full view of various bureaucrats and security personnel who were going through the open rooms visible to all visitors. Gaddafi's "official" security guard was made up of lady parachute "soldiers" who walked around in combat uniforms with high heels and colorful trousers. During this particular meeting, Gaddafi was constantly catching the eyes of these young commando-damsels on the prowl and waving at them quite warmly, as if he were saying, "See you later, sweetie."

At one meeting, Gaddafi turned to me and said, "Mr. Cohen, this will interest you. I am in negotiations with the Libyan Jews who were expelled in 1959 to return to Libya." (The expulsion of Libyan Jews took place before Gaddafi came to power in 1969.) I asked where they had settled. He said that half were in Italy and half had gone to Israel. He appeared to be quite animated by the idea. Flash forward to 2010 during my last visit to Tripoli. I was invited to lecture at the university by the "Organization for the Worldwide Study of the Green Book," Gaddafi's answer to Mao's "Little Red Book." I asked if the Jews had returned. The answer was that some did return. They reclaimed their confiscated property, promptly sold it, and returned to their countries of exile. In July 2012, the Arab language newspaper *Al-Hayat* quoted Gaddafi's chief of protocol, Nuri al-Samara, as saying that Gaddafi's mother was Jewish. Apparently she was an Italian Jew residing in Libya. At age 18, she married a Libyan Arab and converted to Islam, according to al-Samara's statement. Her family in Israel apparently confirmed this report. They said that she visited Israel regularly and distributed money to her Italian Jewish relatives.

In 1987, when all the other Arab leaders, along with other nations, refused to support Gaddafi in his struggle against UN sanctions, he decided that he was no longer primarily an Arab first, but first and foremost an African. He decided to lavish attention on the Organization of African Unity, financing summit meetings at his future capital, Sirte, and investing in businesses around the continent.

During one of our visits to Sirte, we found a mini-African summit in progress. Gaddafi was trying to mediate the conflict between the late President Laurent Kabila of the Congo and President Paul Kagame of Rwanda.

I was in luck. Before I left Washington, I had received an appeal from an American missionary group asking for assistance in obtaining freedom for one of their young missionaries, who had been arrested in the Congo for photographing a forbidden subject, intelligence headquarters. I asked for an audience with Kabila at our hotel. I made my pitch for the missionary. I told him that I knew the young man's parents, who had spent their lives in the Congo helping the sick and the poor. He immediately got on the phone and ordered the man released.

At ten p.m., Steve Hayes and I were called to the all-terrain vehicles for the ride to meet Gaddafi in his tent. We started out on paved roads and then entered dirt roads. Then we proceeded to open terrain with no roads and no lights. In the headlights, we saw small animals dashing around. We finally arrived at Gaddafi's lavish Bedouin tent in the middle of nowhere.

Knowing my background in African diplomacy, Gaddafi spoke proudly of his work to organize the African nations into a unified whole. He talked of his investments in hotels, bus lines, and commercial agriculture. I congratulated him because his assistance to African nations emphasized the private sector as opposed to the traditional aid to governments. His bitterness at being betrayed by his Arab brothers was barely disguised.

In my discussions with African heads of state in the countries immediately adjacent to Libya, I found them somewhat bewildered by Gaddafi. They liked him for his largesse, but they feared him for his quixotic unpredictability. They made sure to stay on his right side.

During one visit to Bamako, the capital of Mali, in 1998, I was there strictly as a private business representative and did not ask to see any government leader. Nevertheless, I saw a protocol officer from the president's palace who brought me a request to meet with President Omar Konare. A good friend, he was Mali's first freely elected president after twenty-five years of military dictatorship, which ended in 1991.

I assumed that Konare wanted my view on the evolution of US policy in Africa. That was not the case. His only interest was in my view of US-Libyan relations. He asked me, "What can be done to normalize US-Libyan relations?"

I told him that the condition set by the United States and the United Kingdom for the removal of UN sanctions against Libya was quite clear. Gaddafi needed to send two suspects in the Lockerbie bombing to The Hague for trial. I told Konare that there was no possible compromise on that.

I then asked him why he was so interested in US-Libyan relations? His reply was that "Libya is our neighbor. One has to get along with one's neighbors." That answer told me how important Gaddafi's influence was on the African countries in his own neighborhood.

Toward the year 2000, Britain and the United States decided to move negotiations forward. There was a UN Security Council resolution offering to lift crippling sanctions if Libya would deliver to justice two intelligence operatives who had been identified as the planners of the Lockerbie PanAm terrorist act. At that point, our discussions with Gaddafi's close advisers were designed to alleviate their fear that the United States would move the goal posts and stab Libya in the back no matter how much they complied with the UN resolution.

OK, they said, the UN resolution promises automatic lifting of UN sanctions against Libya if the two suspects would appear at The Hague for trial by the International Court of Justice. The paranoid Libyans could not believe that the United States would not find a way to fool them. So, they invented the diabolical idea of a reverse veto, as follows. After the two suspects arrived at The Hague, the United States would introduce a resolution calling for the sanctions to continue despite the language of the original resolution. Steve and I protested that such a resolution could not obtain the necessary nine votes for passage. But, our Libyan challengers declared, the United States would then impose a reverse veto, thereby passing the resolution with less than nine votes. It took us three sessions to persuade them that neither the United States nor any other permanent member of the Security Council could exercise a "reverse veto."

Despite our persuasive and persistent arguments, it finally took a visit by Nelson Mandela to convince Gaddafi to send the two suspects to The Hague. Once he had done this, there was considerable relaxation in Libya's international relations. The United States did not remove its sanctions for several more years, until Libya settled compensation claims from the families of the Lockerbie victims. After Gaddafi complied with the UN resolution, I finally went public in a Tripoli press moment in 2002, congratulating him for his decision.

My last encounter with Gaddafi took place in 2009 when the World Affairs Council of the United States invited him to have a dialogue with their members via satellite television. In view of my relationship with the Leader, the Council chairperson asked me to join her in moderating the discussion. The atmosphere was positive. The United States had normalized relations with Libya. We had reopened our embassy in Tripoli. There was nothing wrong with inviting Gaddafi to visit with Americans

The format called for Gaddafi to make a thirty-minute statement and then take questions from the Council sent to the moderators by e-mail. Gaddafi's statement was unsurprising. He emphasized the importance of Arab solidarity. He told the Americans that we are losing influence in the Middle East because of the lack of balance in our view of the Israel-Palestine conflict. He boasted about his support to sub-Saharan African countries. He was the total statesman in his demeanor and speech.

During the discussion period, one question from a woman in California got on his nerves. She said that she had read his famous "Green Book" and had a question about the role of women in a modern society. "Mr. Leader, in your book you say that the proper role for today's woman is to be a mother and caregiver at home. Do you mean to say that women have no role in Libya in the building of a modern society?" Gaddafi became somewhat flustered, but managed to claim that he really did not mean to demean the role of women, without much conviction. He put distance between himself and that issue as fast as he could. On the whole, anyone who had not really followed Gaddafi's antics over the years would have thought from that performance that he was perfectly normal and reasonable.

What we saw in Gaddafi's Libya was an immense tragedy. Walking the streets of Tripoli, as well as driving along the road to Tunisia, we saw dead people walking. There were no smiles anywhere. Despite Libya's immense oil wealth, the vast majority of the people were living slightly above the poverty line. At age 29 in 1969, when Gaddafi seized power, Marxism was the rage among people of his generation in the Middle East, in Africa, and among many groups in Western Europe. In the Middle East, Arab nationalism held equal status with Marxism.

Gaddafi implemented Marxism in his own way, with virtually no private investment outside of the oil sector. Lots of oil money was frittered away in support of revolutionary groups all over the world, from Northern Ireland to the Philippines. Additional funds were invested in small and medium-sized businesses in sub-Saharan Africa in order to gain those nations' support against sanctions. But private business in Libya was essentially prohibited.

Apart from Al Jazeera television broadcasts, the Libyans had absolutely no access to the international media. There were no book outlets, and no kiosks with magazines and newspapers. After sanctions were lifted in 2001, Gaddafi's son Seif al-Islam started a media company and planned to import foreign publications, including the *International Herald Tribune*. Gaddafi's team of elder protectors of the faith made sure the project never got off the ground.

Based on our five intimate meetings and what actually happened as the result of Gaddafi's decisions, are we justified in describing him as "Hitlerian"? I would say yes. He had all the attributes and views: "The Arab nation is superior to all others. Islam is the only true faith. We have the right to eliminate all others." The black Africans are only slightly better than slaves in his view. How different was his "Arab socialism" from Hitler's national socialism? In theory, there was no difference. In practice, thank heaven, Gaddafi lacked the technology and industrial know-how to project his vision of Arab power.

In the day-to-day world of international relations, it was all about Gaddafi, with his "Green Book" and his megalomaniacal antics that gained massive publicity, mostly derisive. But he did not care, as long as the international press talked about him. When the end came in the revolution of 2011–2012, it was hard to find anyone who was sorry to see him go. As for Steve Hayes and me, we had a great time trying to keep Gaddafi amused as we did track-two diplomacy with his close advisers. We were glad to have made a small contribution to the eventual end of Gaddafism.

As for the future of Libya, it is clear, as of late 2014, two years after Gaddafi's demise that the late "Leader" was having his revenge. The vast stocks of conventional arms in his warehouses were being trafficked throughout the African nations in the belt south of the North African Arab states. The civil war and guerrilla insurgency in northern Mali began with the return of Malian mercenaries from their defeat in Libya in early 2012. Within Libya, Gaddafi's policy of divide and rule resulted in multiple conflicts among the country's tribal clans. Gaddafi created no institutions, and the Libyan people have virtually no experience in self-government. The country is facing many years of instability.

Thinking back to 1969 when Gaddafi and his band of young

officers succeeded in their bloodless coup that deposed the reigning King Idris, I remember a discussion in the State Department's Bureau of African Affairs. It was at Assistant Secretary David Newsom's morning staff meeting. I was there as director for Central African Affairs. Hearing the report that Gaddafi had ordered the closing of Wheelus Air Base, the US Air Force operational base on the outskirts of Tripoli, Secretary Newsom said, "I do not think we should accept this edict. We should fight it."

Having recently returned from pre-Gaddafi Libya where he was the US ambassador, Newsom knew the country and the culture very well. The rest of us demurred. We saw Gaddafi's coup as an act of anti-Western nationalism. We felt that the nationalists were unstoppable, as in a number of other Middle Eastern countries. We decided to live with the change and accept the loss of the air force base.

In the following months, we began to receive reports of some immature antics on Gaddafi's part. He was spotted hanging around the American Club in some sort of disguise on a Friday night. We later found out that he was checking on reports that the American teenagers were consuming alcohol. Later, things really became nasty. Because he believed that the hated Israel could not exist without United States support, he wanted to demonstrate his unhappiness with US policy in the Middle East. This took the form of an anti-US demonstration in front of the American Embassy. Not surprisingly, the demonstration got out of hand, and the Embassy building sustained significant damage. Anticipating what might be happening in Washington, he called in our chargé d'affaires, James Blake, and informed him that the government of Libya would pay for all repairs. It did not work. With the loss of the air force base and Gaddafi's visceral anti-American outlook, the Nixon White House decided over David Newsom's objection that the US Embassy in Tripoli would be closed. That was the beginning of a long period of hostility in US-Libyan relations.

In those early days of Gaddafi's rule, we had no way of predicting what sort of an accomplished monster he would become.

The late Mohamed Siad Barre (left) in the capital Mogadishu shortly after taking power in 1969.
Credit: Mogadiscio Images

CHAPTER 11

Mohamed Siad Barre—Somalia

The Ethiopians Are Coming

Historical Note

Mohamed Siad Barre became the absolute ruler of Somalia in October 1969 through a military coup. He remained in power until January 1991, when the entire country fell into a state of unstable anarchy, with local warlords controlling different geographic sectors. Somalia itself had become independent from Italy and the United Kingdom in 1960. The Italian colony of Somalia and the British colony of Somaliland became independent at the same time and merged into a single country within days. Siad Barre had been the army commander until he became the country's president.

Although the people of Somalia share a common language and a common Muslim religion, the majority has a sense of nationhood only when there are external threats. In normal times, Somalis rely first and foremost on their extended family relationships known as clans and subclans. After independence, the major rallying element for the Somali people was their demand for the reunification of all Somalis living in the Horn of Africa under one flag. Significant Somali-speaking populations living under other flags in 1960 were in the Ogaden region of Ethiopia, northeast Kenya, and Djibouti.

As in a number of other African countries under military rule in the 1960s, Siad Barre began his dictatorship as a "scientific socialist," with all major economic activity reserved for the state. The major source of foreign exchange was the massive annual sale of livestock to the Arabian Peninsula, a short distance across the Gulf of Aden. Because of his political ideology, Siad Barre received significant assistance from the Soviet Union.

In 1977, Siad Barre decided to launch an invasion of Ethiopia's

Ogaden region in an effort to annex that Somali-populated region. His initial war effort was successful. But the Ethiopian regime had experienced its own Marxist coup in 1975 and turned to the Soviet Union for support against Somalia. The Soviets decided that Ethiopia was a far greater prize and switched their support from Somalia to Ethiopia. The Soviets sponsored the arrival of 15,000 Cuban troops in Ethiopia in 1978, decisively beating back the Somali invasion. At this point, Siad Barre turned to the United States for support. Having lost its once strong influence in Ethiopia, the United States developed good relations with the Siad Barre regime through major economic development programs and modest military assistance programs.

After his failure to win back the Ogaden, Siad Barre's internal rule became increasingly repressive, with his own Marehan clan gaining increasing control of resources. This led to clan- against-clan violence. Siad Barre's most difficult problem was with the Somalis in the former UK Somaliland, centered on the major city of Hargesa. Increasing repressive violence against the people of Hargesa led to large numbers becoming refugees in Ethiopia.

The internal situation continued to deteriorate throughout the 1980s, with various clan militias taking up arms against the central government. Toward the end of that decade, Siad Barre's realm was reduced mainly to the capital city of Mogadishu. Hargesa refugees in Ethiopia were trained and armed to fight Siad Barre. They entered the civil war in 1989–1990. During this period, Siad Barre and his family embezzled all of the foreign revenue coming in from livestock exports to Aden.

The Siad Barre government collapsed completely in January 1991, and the country's anarchy intensified. The American Embassy was evacuated under emergency conditions with the help of military helicopters diverted from US forces in the Gulf of Aden preparing to oust the Iraqi invaders from Kuwait. Siad Barre escaped to the southeastern Somali port city of Kismayo but was later forced to flee to Lagos, Nigeria, where he died in January 1995.

Between 1991 and 2012, the Somali political and ethnic leaders were unable to establish a credible central authority because of mistrust and corruption pervading the clan system. In 2006, an insurgent group with ties to the terrorist organization al-Qaeda began operating in Somalia and achieved significant territorial gains. This brought in neighboring African military units from Uganda, Burundi, Kenya, and Ethiopia, who subsequently brought the Islamic fighters under control. A fairly credible government was elected in 2012, and there was hope that it might stabilize Somalia with significant international assistance.

During the crisis of the 1980s, the former British Somaliland announced its secession from the Republic of Somalia in two parts, Somaliland and Puntland. As of early 2015, both these entities were operating independently, with Somaliland actually receiving credit for democracy and good governance. Neither entity, however, has received international recognition pending the outcome of the fate of Somalia itself.

The Horn of Africa is separated from the Middle East by the Red Sea and the Gulf of Aden. The countries in the Horn include Sudan, Ethiopia, Eritrea, Kenya, Djibouti, and Somalia. I would claim that the west shore of the Red Sea is not the east coast of Africa. Considering culture, language, and political outlook, I would argue that the Middle East includes the countries in the Horn. One exception would be Kenya, with a Middle Eastern population of less than 10 percent, which resides on the Indian Ocean coast.

Somalia is certainly more of a Middle Eastern country than an African country. Indeed, Somalia joined the Arab League very soon after independence. The mentality is very much the same in Somalia as in the Middle East. Politics are a zero-sum game. To compromise is to show weakness. Nomadic life is insecure and harsh. Don't trust anyone who is not a member of your clan, ethnic group, or extended family. Shoot first and ask questions later.

I began seeing Somalia's military dictator Siad Barre when I started my assignment on the National Security Council in January 1988. I last saw him in mid-1990 as the country was in a state of rapid disintegration.

On most of my visits, Siad Barre received me during the midnight hour. He seemed to be most mentally alert in the middle of the night. During my career, as noted, I found that military regimes were generally more prone to late night meetings than were civilian ones.

After Somalia's 1978 defeat in the Ogaden war against Ethiopia, Siad Barre was totally paranoid about the prospect of attack from Ethiopia. Each time I visited, the first thing he said was a variation of "The Ethiopian army is about to invade Somalia. We need more arms and support from the United States." I remember asking why he was so sure that an Ethiopian attack was imminent. He said that Somali-speaking Ethiopians from the Ogaden region were serving in the Ethiopian Army. His intelligence service had developed agents within the Somali-speaking units. These sources provided reliable evidence of an imminent Ethiopian invasion.

My response was consistent. "The Soviets are the main source of military and financial assistance to the Ethiopian army and air force. The Soviets will not allow the Ethiopians to drag them into an unwinnable war in the desert. What you have to worry about, Mr. President, are the Somali refugees in Ethiopia undergoing military training. These refugees hate you and are waiting to be unleashed against you."

Siad Barre resented the fact that our military assistance to Somalia was designed for defense and not for offense. The Ethiopians were receiving far more heavy combat items from the Soviets than the Somalis were receiving from the United States.

Siad's human rights record made us leery of getting too deeply into his bed with heavy military cooperation. My purpose during my visits was to explore every possibility of reconciliation among the various clans that were at each other's throats. That was extremely difficult with someone like Siad, who did not have a grain of sympathy for his Somali opponents. They might just as well have been nationals of other countries.

In 1989, when anti-Siad insurgents took over the city of Hargesa in what is now secessionist Somaliland, Siad ordered a massive artillery barrage against the city. Thousands of noncombatant civilians were killed. It was hard to envision a similar event happening in what I call the real Africa west and south of the Horn.

In another event, in 1990, Siad decided to attend a soccer match in the Mogadishu stadium. As his vehicle entered the stadium, the crowd gave him a royal booing. His reaction was to order a machine-gunning of the crowd.

While my discussions with Siad were cordial but not terribly productive, he was most comfortable with senior American military officers visiting from the headquarters of the US Central Command in Tampa, Florida. The closer he could come to the protection of the US military, the more secure he felt. Somehow, he felt that if push came to shove, the US military would come to his rescue against internal opponents. He was living in a dream world, but the many visits from Tampa fed his fantasies.

In 1979, the Soviets invaded Afghanistan. This act of aggression infuriated President Jimmy Carter. He ordered the CIA to prepare a program of covert support for Afghan resistance groups. In our close intelligence surveillance of Soviet activities in south Asia, we detected reliable information that the Soviet general staff was planning to use Afghanistan as a springboard for deep incursions south into Iran, Kuwait, and other countries of the Gulf. Having committed aggression against Afghanistan, why not continue on to commit aggression against more valuable territory? "In for a kopek, in for a ruble," as they say in Moscow.

This intelligence was sketchy, but the White House started to panic. How could the United States protect Iran, Kuwait, and other Gulf countries from Soviet military invasion? Our friends in the Gulf region told us they did not want US military forces based in their countries. They wanted us to be available if needed, but we should keep our forces "over the horizon." None of the Muslim nations wanted to have "infidel" soldiers based in their countries.

The White House solution for this challenge was to obtain base rights in neighboring countries in the Horn of Africa. Ambassador Reginald Bartholomew, the assistant secretary of state for political-military affairs, traveled to the Horn of Africa on an urgent diplomatic mission. His diplomacy was quite successful, especially in Somalia.

Fresh from his defeat in Ethiopia, Siad Barre was enthusiastic about entering the American security environment. He granted the United States full access to the port and airport of the coastal city of Berbera on the Gulf of Aden. (This city is now within the secessionist Somaliland.) At the time of Siad Barre, Berbera was the main terminal for the export of livestock to the Arabian Peninsula.

The United States appropriated $50 million for the upgrade of the Berbera port and airport. We never had military personnel there.

Maintenance for the facility was the responsibility of an American company under contract, with only a handful of American personnel. As far as Siad was concerned, Berbera constituted an iron link uniting his regime and the United States. His strong relations with the American military also made it easier for Siad to withstand my pressure for a negotiated settlement with the insurgent clans. In Washington, the Pentagon was consistent in telling us in the State Department how important Berbera was in their planning to protect the Gulf nations from possible Soviet aggression.

The fate of Berbera took an ironic twist during the first Gulf War to defeat Saddam Hussein's aggression against Kuwait in 1990. As soon as Saddam's forces took over Kuwait, all of the countries in the Gulf, except Iran, suddenly wanted US forces on their soil. As a result, none of the facilities negotiated in 1979–1980, in Somalia, Kenya, Djibouti, and Sudan were used in the first Gulf War. Most of our forces were based in Saudi Arabia and Bahrain.

By 1990, Siad was already in deep trouble, and it was clear that he could not remain in power much longer. We called him the "Mayor of Mogadishu." During the second half of that year, he finally informed me that he was ready to negotiate with the rebels, with the United States as mediator. But it was too late. When we contacted the rebels, they refused. Siad was on the ropes, and they were moving in for the kill. Siad escaped from Mogadishu in January 1991, taking refuge in the southern port city of Kismayo, not far from the Kenyan border. When Kismayo fell to the rebels, Siad escaped into Kenya. He finally settled in Lagos, where he died in 1995.

Siad was not unique in that large segment of the northeastern part of the African continent that I consider an extension of the Middle East. His disdain for human life and the ease with which he could order mass murder of his own citizens were in the mainstream of the subregion. I have seen similar policies implemented by heads of state in the Sudan, Ethiopia, and Eritrea.

The late Jonas Savimbi, president of the rebel group National Union for the Total Independence of Angola (UNITA), meeting with President George H. W. Bush in the White House, September 1990.
Credit: White House photo

CHAPTER 12

Jonas Malheiro Savimbi—Angola

Angola's Man of the People

Historical Note

Unlike Britain and France, which agreed to bring their African colonies to independence through a ten-year transition from 1950 to 1960, the authoritarian Portuguese regime headed by Antonio Salazar considered its African colonies to be overseas provinces of Portugal. Hence, independence was out of the question. Hundreds of thousands of Portuguese citizens had moved to Africa to escape crushing unemployment and poverty at home. Angola, Mozambique, Guinea-Bissau, Cape Verde, and São Tomé had to remain part of Portugal through economic necessity.

Unfortunately for the Lisbon government, after the year 1960 the newly independent former British, French, and Belgian colonies bordering on the Portuguese territories were more than willing to assist nationalist movements seeking independence from Portugal. As a result, Portugal was faced with armed guerrilla movements in all of their colonies and had to go to great expense in blood and treasure to keep them under control.

It was against this background of anti-Portuguese wars that Jonas Savimbi became a freedom fighter in his home nation of Angola. Educated in Portugal and Switzerland and trained in guerrilla warfare in Maoist China, Savimbi took up arms against Portugal in 1966. That began his three-decade quest for the presidency of Angola.

Unlike Mozambique on Africa's southeast coast, where the anti-Portuguese nationalist movement was unified within one party, Angola's nationalists were divided into three warring groups. The Popular Movement for the Liberation of Angola (MPLA) was linked to the clandestine Communist Party of Portugal and received support from the Marxist government of the Republic of Congo (Brazzaville). The National Front for the Liberation of Angola (FNLA) was tied closely to President Mobutu of Zaire and was therefore considered to be pro-West.

Unable to find compatibility with either of the two groups, Savimbi started his own guerrilla group that he called the National Union for the Total Independence of Angola (UNITA). Initially, UNITA's main source of cross-border support came from independent Zambia on Angola's eastern border. In view of his training in China, Savimbi was initially considered to be a fervent Maoist, and, indeed, he received material assistance from China.

Between 1960 and 1974, the United States could do little to encourage intransigent Portugal to reconsider its opposition to independence for its African colonies. Portugal was a NATO ally and allowed the US military to use a major air force base in the Azores archipelago. But everything changed suddenly in 1974, when the government in Lisbon was overthrown by the military, thus ending four decades of corporatist dictatorship.

The younger military officers who took power were determined to move Portugal to a democratic transition, a policy that succeeded. As to the African colonies, the officers decided that immediate independence was the answer. Needless to say, this decision wreaked havoc within the colonies. Hundreds of thousands of Portuguese citizens returned to Portugal as refugees, causing a tremendous burden on an already poor society.

Within the colonies, dominant nationalist movements were able to take power and begin the difficult task of establishing viable states without any preparation. The exception was Angola, where three independence movements found themselves unable to agree on power sharing and had no option but to continue the fight for control against each other. It was at this point that the three leaders looked to the outside world for support, and Jonas Savimbi began to be taken seriously.

Over the years, I have known many African leaders who desperately wanted to be heads of state. But none of them lusted for high power more than Jonas Savimbi, the man who could not become president of Angola despite thirty-five years of political and military combat.

Savimbi came to international attention in the aftermath of regime change in Portugal in 1974. The immediate granting of independence to Angola, without any organized political transition, left that country with three guerrilla movements vying for national power. How that fight was resolved caught Washington's attention in a big way.

The communist-linked MPLA made the audacious decision to ask Cuba for military assistance. This was Fidel Castro's opportunity to thumb his nose at the United States and show the world that Cuba was not taking orders from the Soviet Union. In November 1975, Cuba airlifted 5,000 troops to Angola and quickly installed the MPLA in power in the capital city, Luanda.

The Cuban forces' superiority in weapons forced the FNLA in northern Angola to move back across the border to Zaire for safety. Similarly, UNITA under Jonas Savimbi was forced to retreat to Angola's far southeast. Not to be outdone by their Cuban junior partner, the Soviet Union began a massive military support program to assist the MPLA in developing its own national army.

Needless to say, Washington was both unhappy and embarrassed. President Gerald Ford declared that the policy of détente between the United States and the Soviet Union was dead. Secretary of State Kissinger's first reaction was to begin covert actions to provide arms and technical assistance to the FNLA and UNITA in order to begin harassing the Cubans and their Angolan allies. Kissinger's action was cut short by the Democratic majority in Congress, which strongly opposed new international adventures so soon after the end of the Vietnam War. Congress enacted legislation, known as the Clark Amendment, prohibiting all US assistance to any group in Angola. The United States was reduced to being a bystander, and Jonas Savimbi was left to welcome support from racist South Africa, which was able to keep his movement alive, but just barely.

It was at this point that Jonas Savimbi began his long struggle to achieve international recognition as the authentic pro-Western freedom fighter against the Marxist Angolan regime and its Cuban and Soviet supporters. With the help of South African–financed

American public relations firms, Savimbi totally seduced the right wing of the American political spectrum. It was during this period of Savimbi's growing popularity in the United States that I started to interact with him seriously.

My first contacts with Savimbi took place during 1965–1966 in Lusaka, Zambia, where I was the economic officer, and from 1977 to 1980 in Dakar, Senegal, where I was the US ambassador. In Lusaka, I saw Savimbi on the cocktail party circuit. At that time, the Portuguese were still in control in Angola, and Savimbi was the anti-colonial hero in Zambia. There were strong cross-border ethnic ties, and Savimbi spoke fluent English. For the Zambians, Savimbi represented the independence struggle. During social conversations, I found Savimbi to be modest, soft-spoken, and entirely diplomatic. He said that he loved the Portuguese people he had known in Angola, but the "fascist" regime in Lisbon did not understand the historical changes that were taking place in Africa.

After the MPLA had taken power in Angola with Cuban military support, Senegalese president Léopold Senghor invited Savimbi to set up a UNITA office in Dakar, because he considered Savimbi to be the true "African" leader of the Angolan people. The MPLA leaders were more Portuguese than African, in Senghor's view. Angola's president, Agostinho Neto, and all of his ministers, could not speak African languages. Senghor saw them as being culturally Portuguese.

It was later, during Savimbi's periodic visits to Dakar, that I had an opportunity to meet him and have serious conversations with him. I found him to be one of the most charismatic and sophisticated African leaders whom I had the pleasure to meet. He spoke English and French with full fluency. Sitting next to him at a dinner party, my wife Suzanne, who is French, said that she considered Savimbi's fluency in French to be almost perfect.

Savimbi also demonstrated his deep knowledge of the Angolan people, especially the agricultural populations from his home area on the central plateau. He spoke with passion about their suffering under the Portuguese and their new repression under the Marxist regime of the MPLA. He was very persuasive.

When I asked Savimbi about the hated *apartheid* regime in South Africa being UNITA's main source of support, he said that he had to take his assistance from whatever source was available. Naturally, he deplored the absence of support from the United States and Western Europe in his struggle to overcome Cuban and Soviet influence over the MPLA regime.

Savimbi's father was an Evangelical Protestant pastor in an overwhelmingly Roman Catholic nation. With this background, and with his own personal charm, Savimbi was able to win the confidence and support of conservative and evangelical constituencies in the United States. During the first half of the 1980s, Savimbi made many trips to the United States, picking up increasing political support with each visit. The "liberal" side of the American political spectrum remained suspicious because of his close relationship with the white South African military and intelligence services.

In 1986, President Ronald Reagan announced his doctrine designed to counter the previously announced "Brezhnev Doctrine" of the Soviet president, which had pledged support to "socialist revolutionary" forces throughout the world. The Reagan Doctrine said that the United States would work to support "democratic nations" facing destabilization from socialist revolutionaries. Only three years away from the fall of the Berlin wall, the Cold War continued to be the most important element of American foreign policy.

In view of the substantial Cuban military presence in Angola, it was no surprise when the Reagan administration designated Angola as the first target of his doctrine in 1986. The Democratic Party leadership did not consider it prudent to oppose him in view of the strong feelings in the United States about Cuba. Reagan requested the repeal of the Clark Amendment that forbade the provision of aid to any party in Angola. The repeal had the support of Democratic members of Congress, and the first order of business after that was the organization of a CIA "covert action" project to support UNITA. On the other hand, the liberals obtained a reciprocal concession. In 1986 the Congress also enacted significant economic sanctions against *apartheid* South Africa.

The beginning of US support gave Savimbi full legitimacy in the Western world, and he used it to move within high political circles to develop strong links. In the United States, Savimbi concentrated on the Protestant Evangelical communities in Texas, Louisiana, and Oklahoma. He was riding high in those friendly environments.

During 1987 and 1988, the State Department concentrated on a marathon negotiation involving Angola, South Africa, and Cuba designed to remove Cuban and South African troops. While this was going on, UNITA was in its corner in southeast Angola working on its capability to ward off Angolan air and armor offensive strikes. CIA equipment was relatively uncomplicated—shoulder-fired ground-to-air missiles to keep the Angolan air force from flying at low altitudes and Milan anti-tank missiles to stop the Angolan armor. This effectively gave UNITA the ability to stop the Angolan government offensives against them but did not give them a capability of striking back with strong blows. In effect, US assistance was limited to keeping UNITA from being defeated.

Savimbi used the 1987–1988 period to travel extensively and develop strong links with democratic forces. He was the Angolan striving for democracy in a struggle against the Marxist minority regime in power. As President Reagan's special assistant for African affairs, I saw a lot of him, as did many State Department officials and members of Congress. At all times, he told us what we wanted to hear. He was for a democratic solution in Angola. He wanted to become president of Angola, but only through free and fair elections.

Savimbi was wined and dined in Washington, with strong help from the embassy of Côte d'Ivoire, the Heritage Foundation, and the embassy of South Africa. He had a strong UNITA representative in Washington named Tito Chingunji, who was almost as charming and persuasive as Savimbi himself. All of their movements and activities in Washington and the rest of the United States were professionally coordinated by American lobbying firms financed by South Africa.

After the signing of the New York treaty of December 1988 that set the stage for the independence of Namibia and the departure of Cuban and South African troops from Angola, our first problems with Savimbi began.

After I became assistant secretary of state for African affairs in 1989, I decided the time was ripe to encourage a win-win peace between the Angolan government and UNITA. The government needed an end to UNITA's guerrilla war. UNITA needed an opportunity to compete for power through a democratic transition.

The Angolan people needed an end to thirty years of humanitarian disaster.

Since we were providing direct assistance to UNITA, we could not pretend to be neutral. So, we asked Angola's neighbors to take the lead in bringing the parties together. This resulted in the organization of an African summit meeting in Zaire at President Mobutu's provincial residence of Gbadolite, roughly 800 miles north of Kinshasa. It was August 1989.

Savimbi did not want to participate. He felt that he would be overwhelmed by the heads of state, who would naturally want to favor their Angolan counterpart, Jose Eduardo Dos Santos. I felt that we had a unique opportunity to end the civil war. In any event, the heads of state were acting upon our request. We could not allow the effort to be aborted. I decided to call Côte d'Ivoire president Félix Houphouët-Boigny, who was Savimbi's mentor and best friend in sub-Saharan Africa. Houphouët agreed with my argument and persuaded Savimbi to show up in Gbadolite.

The summit meeting drew eighteen heads of state, along with Savimbi and President Dos Santos of Angola. After one day of deliberations, a "consensus" emerged. Savimbi would become vice president of Angola under the existing constitution. UNITA would become a legitimate political party, thereby making Angola a multiparty state. Savimbi would be a candidate for the presidency in the next election.

Since the United States was not providing the type of military support to UNITA that would help them win their guerrilla war, I reached the conclusion that the consensus proposal at the summit meeting was about as good as Savimbi could expect. It was a Sunday afternoon when the news came in. I was preparing press guidance that expressed approval of the deal. Savimbi and Dos Santos had both signed off on it, as did the attending heads of state.

Before I could complete the press guidance, I received a call from the office of Secretary of State James Baker saying that I should issue a press statement expressing disapproval of any accord that did not call for a free and fair election in Angola. Savimbi's representative in Washington had called Baker. Savimbi signed the agreement—how could he not sign with eighteen heads of state urging him to do so?—but he did not like the agreement and wanted the United

States to denounce it. The fact that he could instruct his lobbyist to contact Secretary Baker on a Sunday afternoon and dictate US policy reflected his remarkable influence on a large segment of the American body politic.

I followed orders, of course, and President Mobutu of Zaire, who had organized the meeting and put his prestige on the line, was not happy with his friends in Washington. But he said nothing, because he fully expected Savimbi to implement the deal that he had signed. About a week later, my wife and I flew off to Basel, Switzerland, to begin a five-day vacation cruise on the Rhine River to Amsterdam. Her sister and brother-in-law met us there. The day before we were scheduled to board the boat, the State Department called to say that Savimbi was requesting a meeting with me. He suggested that we meet in Rabat, Morocco.

I decided to fly to Rabat because I needed to know what Savimbi was thinking, in view of his lobbyist's action in Washington. I made arrangements to meet the boat in Heidelberg thirty-six hours into the voyage.

Savimbi's approach was to appeal to my democratic instincts. He said that he had been fighting for many years against Portuguese fascism and the MPLA's communism. He did not want to sacrifice his struggle on behalf of the majority of Africans in Angola in order to give his stamp of approval to, and participate in, a Marxist government. He wanted my approval to ignore the Gbadolite accord and continue fighting.

I said, "Mr. President, whatever option you choose, the United States will continue to support UNITA. My only request is that you inform President Mobutu and that you do not rely on me to do it." Savimbi agreed. Shortly thereafter, a gentleman from Moroccan protocol came by to request that I come to the palace to brief His Majesty King Hassan. He was one of the few African leaders who supported Savimbi and maintained a lively interest in Angola.

After I finished briefing the king, he thanked me and said that he wanted to express a grievance. North Africa used to be covered in the State Department within the Bureau of African Affairs. When Henry Kissinger became secretary of state, he transferred jurisdiction over North Africa to the Near East Bureau. His Majesty then pleaded for a return to the Africa Bureau, where Morocco used to carry a lot of weight. In the Near East Bureau, all attention was focused on the Israel-Palestine dilemma. North Africa was essentially ignored. Needless to say, I was unable to fulfill the king's wish, although I would have been happy to expand my jurisdiction.

When Savimbi informed Mobutu that he renounced the Gbadolite accord, all hell broke loose. The summit meeting and the agreement constituted Mobutu's moment of glory. He had become an African statesman. Mobutu fumed and then announced that CIA flights to Savimbi's headquarters in Jamba in southeastern Angola would no longer be allowed to land at Kamina airport in eastern Congo. This effectively stopped the movement of all supplies to UNITA and seriously jeopardized the organization's ability to stave off military assaults from the Angolan government forces. Within two months, both the CIA and the Defense Department informed us that UNITA was in deep trouble.

Our only recourse, at that point was to ask both Mobutu and Savimbi to come to Washington to meet with President Bush. They came and had separate meetings with the president.

Bush spoke to Mobutu as an old friend, dating back to the days when Bush was the United States permanent representative to the United Nations. He said that both Zaire and the United States had worked hard to keep the flame of democracy alive in Angola and that UNITA remained the main hope for change. He hoped that Mobutu's unhappiness with Savimbi's action would not result in a total loss of UNITA's viability.

Mobutu responded that the United States was Zaire's strongest supporter and that he particularly valued President Bush's long friendship. He said that he could not refuse the president's request. As a sign of his sincerity, he would invite Savimbi to come to his sixtieth birthday party at his villa in Cap Martin on the French Riviera two weeks hence. He also said that he wanted Secretary Cohen to be present in order to witness the reconciliation. Mobutu said that he would give the order to allow the CIA flights to start up again. Immediately thereafter, I met with Jim Woods, my counterpart in the Pentagon, and our friend in the CIA to arrange for a surge of equipment to help UNITA eliminate its arms and ammunition deficit.

President Bush then informed Savimbi, who was delighted but

suspicious. The CIA flights were already four months in arrears, and UNITA's situation was becoming desperate. Nevertheless, he welcomed the invitation to the birthday celebration. Two weeks later, Savimbi and I arrived in Paris on separate flights on a Sunday morning. We boarded Mobutu's chartered private jet to Nice and drove to Mobutu's Italianate villa. The birthday party was lavish and joyful. On the way back to the airport afterward, Savimbi said, "I think Mobutu is sincere. He really wants reconciliation."

Between September 1989 and March 1990, UNITA was able to increase its harassment of the Angolan regime. The CIA had trained several sapper teams that were successful in penetrating areas around the capital city of Luanda and destroying various types of infrastructure. The regime's increased frustration and embarrassment formed a prelude to Secretary of State James Baker's meeting with President Dos Santos in Namibia in March.

The occasion was the solemn ceremony marking the independence of the new Republic of Namibia, a large territory sitting between Angola and South Africa. During the Reagan administration, Assistant Secretary of State for Africa Chester Crocker had achieved a triumphal negotiation, resulting in Namibia's independence and the departure of Cuban and South African troops from Angola. The US delegation was thus clearly the star of the show.

Baker told Dos Santos that American assistance to UNITA was not designed to help the rebel group overthrow his regime. On the contrary, US assistance was designed to prevent UNITA's defeat. Baker said that the time had come to seek a negotiated settlement that could lead to a free and fair election. Dos Santos agreed. He said that a mediator was needed. Baker said that the United States obviously could not be the mediator but was available to provide appropriate assistance. Dos Santos asked Baker to obtain Savimbi's agreement.

After the Namibia celebrations, I sent a message to Savimbi asking that he meet Baker in Kinshasa. Ambassador William Harrop in Kinshasa sent back a message indicating that Savimbi would be available. Baker and his party flew to Kinshasa to meet with Savimbi.

When Baker told Savimbi that Dos Santos had agreed to a negotiation leading to a free and fair election, Savimbi did not hesitate. "A free and fair election is what I have been fighting for all of these years. I agree wholeheartedly."

Negotiations under Portuguese mediation started in June 1990 and ended with an agreement in May 1991. The agreement called for an eighteen-month transition period, encampment of troops on both sides, and a free and fair election in September 1992. In the meantime, Savimbi moved into a luxurious villa in the capital city a few houses down from the American Embassy.

During this period, I visited regularly to make sure the transition was on track. Each time, I found Savimbi supremely confident. He knew that he was the most popular because he was the only true African among the political leaders. I worked with him to develop a strategy to make sure the regime did not cheat on the vote count. We arranged for UNITA to have mobile communications from every voting place to their central headquarters. In that way, they could verify the central count done by the independent electoral commission.

As the transition proceeded, I noted that Savimbi's self-confidence was turning into arrogance. His entourage began to treat him as a head of state in waiting. The informality of our relationship turned into formality. I was kept waiting in the outer office for long periods before he arrived for our conversations. We sometimes met in Abidjan in the residence of Côte d'Ivoire president Houphouët-Boigny. At all of our meetings, Houphouët presided, and Savimbi basked in his sponsorship and protection.

During the transition, a horrible event took place at Savimbi's headquarters in Jamba in southeastern Angola. UNITA's representative in Washington, Tito Chingunji, had been recalled to Jamba for consultations. He had been the UNITA representative in Washington for over a decade and was very popular. One day, word arrived that Tito had been assassinated in a voodoo-type ritual. This news caused tremendous consternation in Washington. Secretary Baker was so upset that he had me draft a tough letter to Savimbi that leaked to the press. Baker wanted the world to know that we would not tolerate such behavior. Tito's death sent us a message. Savimbi had become so arrogant that he could not tolerate any competition for public admiration. It left a decided sour taste.

Early in the transition, President Bush and Soviet president

Gorbachev decided to endorse the process and have Dos Santos and Savimbi invited to Washington. Dos Santos, for the first time, would be received at the White House. Savimbi would be received at the Soviet Embassy. When they were both in Washington, Savimbi suddenly had misgivings about going to the Soviet Embassy. I asked him what his problem was. After some hesitation, he said he was afraid that he would be poisoned. He said, "You know, they have poisons that don't act until a few weeks later. They will poison me, and they will escape the blame." I assured him that it would not happen, and his visit with the Soviet ambassador went well.

For the first half of the transition, Savimbi had indeed been the most popular, according to independent polling. But as the campaign went into its second half, Savimbi's lead among voters started to slip badly. His mistake was to campaign as a guerrilla warrior with guns and a rhetoric that emphasized revenge. This scared the voters. President Dos Santos campaigned as a regular guy, with posters showing him playing soccer with school children. The people had had enough of war. They did not warm to Savimbi's warrior rhetoric. At one point in the campaign, Savimbi warned all those who had participated in the black market that they would be punished. Since the only way to survive in urban Angola in those days of extreme socialism was to buy and sell on the black market, Savimbi's remarks frightened virtually every Angolan voter.

The election took place in September 1992. By mutual agreement, the United Nations was the official arbiter as to the election's fairness and legitimacy. UNITA had its people at every polling place, and they signed off on every vote count. When the final official results came in, Dos Santos had 49 percent and Savimbi 34 percent. The agreement called for a runoff in the event none of the candidates obtained a majority. I was in Rome witnessing the signing of the Mozambique peace agreement, to which we had made a major contribution, when the news came in that Savimbi was not accepting the election. His basic message was, "If I did not win, it must be a fraud."

I got on the phone from Rome demanding to speak to Savimbi, but he would not take my call. I spoke to his senior lieutenants recommending that they allow the UN to make an investigation of voting irregularities, as stipulated in the peace agreement, before making rash statements. I made a press statement saying the same things. When the press asked Savimbi's spokesman if they were going to follow Secretary Cohen's advice, the response was "Secretary Cohen can go to hell."

I flew down to Luanda with the chief mediator, Portuguese deputy foreign minister José Manuel Barroso, and met with Savimbi. He was adamant that the election was a fraud and must be overturned. Meeting with Savimbi's lieutenants, I asked what evidence they had of fraud. They showed me a few tally sheets that gave the exact same scores to two minor candidates in several polling places. I told them that evidence was very skimpy, and in any case, they should wait for the UN to investigate their allegations.

During that same visit, I had a conversation with President Dos Santos. He told me that he had been worried that Savimbi might not accept the result. For that reason, he had pleaded with the Portuguese chairman of the independent election commission to lower his own total from 51 percent to 49 percent, the only result made public, so that Savimbi could have an opportunity to contest the election for a second time in a runoff. Savimbi went back to war before a runoff election could take place.

My relationship with Savimbi and UNITA soon reached an unfriendly finale. Savimbi's lieutenants made a formal request that the United States officially denounce the election as fraudulent and demand a rerun. They were used to the United States agreeing to their every request for support since 1986. I told them that I could not do that, because the agreement they signed in Lisbon stipulated that the United Nations and not the United States or any other government would determine the fairness and legitimacy of the election. They argued that the United States could override the UN. I told them flatly that we would not denounce the election as a fraud merely because the wrong person won. At that point, our relationship was over. UNITA decided they would do everything possible to go over my head in Washington. Savimbi and I never spoke again. They were not used to losing any political battles in Washington.

When I returned to Washington, I was surprised at the mild reaction from Savimbi's once- fervent conservative supporters. Arizona senator Dennis DeConcini, for example, told me, "We gave Savimbi what he was asking for, a free and fair election. Our job is done. He no longer deserves our support." Secretary Baker told me that with the end of the Cold War, UNITA was no longer a hot political issue in the US Congress. We were smart to cut a deal when we did. We needed to forget about UNITA.

Some of UNITA's friends, however, did not give up. For months, I regularly came under attack from the Heritage Foundation. Especially virulent was Paul Weyrich, head of the Free Congress Foundation, who said that I had betrayed a great pro-West patriot.

Following the election, UNITA went back to war. It was interesting from the perspective of a conflict mediator to observe how the two sides anticipated the result of the election. While he was sure of victory, Savimbi hedged against the possibility of defeat. During his campaign travels throughout Angola, he had been accompanied by armed security pursuant to the original peace agreement. As he traveled, he managed to infiltrate armed units into strategic locations. In effect, the election campaign allowed him to move fighters outside of the confines of his base camp in southeast Angola into locations around the country.

Also in accordance with the peace agreement, the two armies were sent into encampments. This was accomplished through the good work of the Air National Guard of Arizona. Within the UNITA encampment, the troops quickly started vegetable gardens and made sure they stayed together as cohesive fighting units. They were used to living in the bush. The government army encampments, on the other hand, quickly deteriorated. The troops were used to living with their families in the cities. Since the war was over, they left the camps and went home. The net result was that when UNITA resumed the war, it had a significant advantage. Its troops made significant gains for the first four months after the war restarted, but the government forces were able to re-establish their superiority with the assistance of Soviet arms.

The lesson for us as mediators was to examine closely the motivations of governments and insurgents who sign peace agreements. There are times when peaceful transitions can enable protagonists to rest and prepare for a return to hostilities. Signatures on peace agreements are not always sincere.

The ten years of fighting after the 1992 election caused more hardship to the Angolan people than the war between 1966 and 1991. After a number of cease-fires, it was clear that Savimbi could not accept less than the type of victory that would make him president of Angola. In the end, the Angolan army ambushed and killed him in 2002.

After hearing the news, I had mixed emotions. Absorbing his charm and sophistication over the years, as well as his legitimate claim to be the only real African in the mix of freedom fighters, I felt that he should have been president of Angola. But after seeing the growth of his egomania and authoritarian arrogance over the years, I knew in my heart that the Angolan people had been spared the rule of a tyrannical disciple of Mao Zedong.

GROUP V

The Liberians:
The Tragedy of America's Orphan

The late president Samuel Kenyon Doe of the Republic of Liberia (left) being greeted at the Pentagon by Secretary of Defense Caspar Weinberger {right) in April 1982. *Credit: AMREN.com*

Charles Taylor, the former president of the Republic of Liberia, at his trial for war crimes before the Special Tribunal for Sierra Leon in The Netherlands, 2013.
Credit lbtimes.co.uk

CHAPTER 13

Samuel Doe and Charles Taylor

Two Men Who Set Liberia Back
a Hundred Years

Historical Note

The Republic of Liberia, on the Atlantic coast of Africa's western bulge, was officially proclaimed and recognized as an independent state in 1847. Starting in 1820, Liberia was the destination of thousands of former American slaves who voluntarily agreed to start new lives in Africa achieving their freedom in the United States. A charitable organization, the American Colonization Society, assisted this exodus financially. A number of American political, business, and religious leaders at the time sincerely believed that former slaves would never be able to adapt to living as free people in the United States and that they would be better off living in the homeland of their ancestors.

Because of their more advanced technology and culture, the former Americans who settled in the new nation of Liberia were able to dominate the indigenous African ethnic groups who had been living there for centuries. The former Americans came to be known as "Americo-Liberians," while the indigenous Africans were known as "country people." It was not until 1904 that the "country people" were admitted to Liberian citizenship.

Americo-Liberian rule continued unabated until 1980, when a bloody military coup, led by Master Sergeant Samuel Doe, overthrew the government of President William Tolbert. Doe and his colleagues established the People's Redemption Council, which named Doe president of Liberia. Since Doe was one of the "country people," his becoming president was initially quite popular among

Liberia's majority, who had suffered discrimination and segregation under Americo-Liberian rule.

After a few years, however, it was clear that Doe was channel-
ing wealth and power to his own Krahn ethnic group while ignoring all the others. The Krahns represented only about 10 percent of
the Liberian population, and Doe's popularity diminished rapidly.
In 1985, he had to rig the presidential election to stay in power.
Despite his tribalism and corruption, Doe had good relations with
the United States, which valued his support for US foreign policy.

In December 1989, a band of about two hundred Liberian guerrilla fighters entered Liberia in Nimba County, coming from neighboring Côte d'Ivoire. These fighters had been trained and equipped
in Libya and assisted in their transit to Liberia by the governments
of Burkina Faso and Côte d'Ivoire. Their leader was a former Liberian civil servant named Charles Taylor. This invasion triggered a
destructive civil war that drew in troops from several West African
countries, including Nigeria, Ghana, Guinea, and Sierra Leone. The
war ended in 1996. An election supervised by the United Nations
resulted in Charles Taylor's becoming president in 1997.

Not content with his victory in Liberia, in 1999 President Taylor decided to provide support to rebels in Sierra Leone, the Revolutionary United Front (RUF). In this war, Taylor became a major
player in a war of blood diamonds, trading guns for diamonds
looted by the RUF. At the same time, an anti-Taylor guerrilla movement was established in neighboring Guinea, Liberians United for
Reconciliation and Democracy (LURD). This war, too, was quite
devastating to the peoples of Liberia and Sierra Leone.

In 2003, the Special Tribunal for Sierra Leone indicted Taylor for
war crimes, based on his support for the trade in "blood diamonds"
that caused tremendous human suffering in Sierra Leone. In that
same year, under military pressure from LURD, Taylor resigned
the presidency of Liberia and took refuge in Nigeria. In 2005 Nigeria handed him over to the special tribunal, which convicted him in
2011 for war crimes in Sierra Leone. In September 2013, the international court in the Netherlands upheld Taylor's fifty-year sentence.

In 2005, meanwhile, a free and fair election in Liberia brought
Mrs. Ellen Johnson Sirleaf to power. A noted banker and econo-
mist, President Sirleaf had been active in opposition to both Doe

and Taylor. Her election gave Liberia an opportunity to begin re-construction of its infrastructure and institutions after fifteen years of destructive civil war. She was reelected in 2011.

Liberians consider themselves to be culturally and spiritually close to the United States. Middle class Liberians send their children to study in the States, and the Liberian diaspora community in the United States is large, widespread, and quite successful as professionals in a variety of fields.

Samuel Doe

I first met Samuel Doe in January 1987, when I had just begun an assignment to the National Security Council in the Reagan White House as senior director for Africa and special assistant to the president. I received a call from the State Department informing me that Secretary of State George P. Shultz would be making a tour of five African countries, and I was invited to join his traveling party.

Our first stop was Monrovia, Liberia. President Doe had been in office seven years. His relations with the United States were excellent. Liberia's support for US positions in UN voting was almost 100 percent. Liberia also supported the United States against attacks by other African governments during debates within the Organization of African Unity. Liberia was a major recipient of American foreign aid, mainly military. The United States had both a giant diplomatic communications base and a Voice of America relay station in the outskirts of Monrovia. The rent payments were minimal. We also had full and unrestricted military access to the Roberts Field International Airport, managed by Pan American World Airways under contract.

The first event was a meeting between Doe and Shultz in the presidential palace. The two principals sat on opposite sides of an oval table. The rest of us, American and Liberian officials, sat about twenty-five feet away in rows of chairs, as in a theater.

After the conversation had been underway for about a minute, I could not believe what I was witnessing. President Doe had worked himself up to a high-pitched scream that was defaulting to a whine every few sentences. This thirty-seven-year-old master-sergeant-turned-president was having a tantrum like a six-year-old child.

"Washington does not appreciate what we are doing for you in support of American foreign policy. You give far more aid to countries like Tanzania that do not support the US. I receive insults from other Africans for our loyalty to the US. You are taking us for granted," and on and on.

Totally unperturbed, Shultz tried to explain that the US Congress was becoming increasingly impatient with the absence of accountability in the Liberian budgetary process. Indeed, there was no Liberian budget. Revenue from the lucrative international ship registry (foreign flags) program, as well as from natural rubber exports, was disappearing. The Liberian government needed to install some fiscal controls or the Congress would cut them off.

A key member of Shultz's party was Dr. Peter McPherson, administrator of the US Agency for International Development (US-AID). McPherson tried to appease Doe by saying he had a structural problem due mainly to inexperience. It was not a question of dishonesty. Doe needed help to set up a system that would allow him and everyone else to know where incoming revenue was coming from and how it was being spent. He proposed to send a team of experts to Monrovia to work with Doe's finance officials and set up that system. They would remain in Monrovia as long as it took to do the job right.

Doe agreed, and it looked like bilateral relations would remain excellent. Nevertheless, in addition to growing congressional unhappiness with US aid being "wasted" in Liberia, the Reagan administration also had to worry about criticism from human rights groups and Liberians living in the United States, all of whom considered Doe to be a monster who should be isolated. Doe had no friends within the US Liberian community, especially among the Americo-Liberians, who had lost their dominant power in the 1980 coup. Indeed, they were ashamed of the guy. They considered him to be an ignorant peasant with zero intellectual depth.

After our meeting with Doe, there was a gala lunch in Shultz's honor. At this event, I felt transported to the American antebellum South. There were prayers, invocations, and choir singing. It was *Gone with the Wind* déjà vu. I felt transported back in time. It was clear that the country boy who had overthrown the minority Americo-Liberians from their traditional hold on power was himself doing his best to emulate the Americo-Liberians.

When we left Monrovia after two days, the departure ceremonies saw Shultz enthroned as a tribal chief with full robes. I felt a certain satisfaction that these people who were longing to be Americans did recognize their African side after all.

Three months later, in April 1987, I received a call from my good friend James Bishop, the US ambassador to Monrovia. Jim explained that the technical team sent by Peter McPherson had been in Monrovia for two months and was totally frustrated. Doe was failing to implement any of the reforms and new budgetary structures. It was not that he was saying one thing and doing another. It was that he was unable to change his practices, which were tied to tribal and family loyalties. Jim asked me to come to Monrovia to leverage my position in the White House to talk sense to President Doe.

I agreed without hesitation and arrived on Bishop's doorstep. We went to see Doe together, and I made my pitch about the need for discipline and fairness to the Liberian people. Doe listened politely and affirmatively. He promised to do the right thing. At the end he asked for a special favor. He said that he was completing studies for a master's degree in political science at the University of Liberia and wondered if I would be his academic sponsor for his thesis. I agreed wholeheartedly. It was rather satisfying to be the mentor of a head of state.

A month later, Ambassador Bishop informed me that my last-minute appeal had failed. Doe was incorrigible. He continued to consider all sources of state revenue to be comingled with his own private bank accounts. He also liked state enterprises to deliver cash to his office in large quantities almost daily. The USAID experts would be going home, mission not accomplished.

Fast forward to Christmas 1989. By this time, I had been in charge of Africa policy as assistant secretary of state for about nine months. I had not heard much from Liberia. US-Liberian relations continued as before. We were all in despair at the absence of good governance but happy to have our facilities and access, while enjoying Liberian support in the international world.

On Christmas day, news came through of an invasion of Liberia by a band of about two hundred fighters coming from Côte d'Ivoire into Nimba County in northeastern Liberia. Nimba was home to the Gio and Mano ethnic groups, who were suffering from discrimination by Doe's regime. The locals thus did not reject the incoming fighters. On the contrary, the small band started to pick up new recruits as they moved inland.

Intelligence reports told us that the leader was a certain Charles Taylor, who had been Doe's chief of general services until he was accused of embezzling state funds in 1987. He escaped to the United States, where he was held in prison awaiting extradition papers from Liberia that never arrived. He "escaped" from his Massachusetts prison, went to Ghana, and thence to Libya via Burkina Faso. Trained in Libya with his band of followers, Taylor had invaded Liberia with the purpose of overthrowing Doe and his regime. He called his movement the National Patriotic Front of Liberia (NPFL).

The first problem we had to face in the midst of this invasion was the comportment of the Liberian army. They immediately started to commit gross human rights violations as they sought to stop the invaders. Whenever enemy fighters were spotted in a Liberian village, the army burned down the entire village and killed many of the villagers. Their purpose was not to win hearts and minds. Needless to say, the more atrocities the army committed, the more young men joined Charles Taylor.

Ambassador Bishop recommended that American military attachés at the embassy be deployed with Liberian army units as observers to discourage human rights violations. I agreed. I did not, however, anticipate the political storm that would erupt when this action became public in the United States. The entire Liberian diaspora started calling their congressional representatives to accuse the US government of sending "advisors" to help Doe stay in power. There was no way we could convince anyone that our purpose was only to help avoid atrocities. When we began receiving angry congressional phone calls, we withdrew the military attachés from the Liberian army units.

Hating Doe as much as they did, the Liberian diaspora adopted Charles Taylor as Liberia's savior without really knowing much about him. Full-page ads appeared in the *Washington Post* and other major newspapers hailing Taylor as God's gift to Liberia. There was no way we could demonstrate any positive feeling for Doe as the legitimate ruler of Liberia at that point.

My next contact with Doe was his phone call asking what we intended to do about the armed incursion. He was clearly hoping for a US intervention on his behalf. After all, Taylor had been trained and financed by Libya's Gaddafi. I told him that he needed to think about a political solution, since Taylor was picking up support from the population as he advanced. Doe said he would send a delegation to see us in Washington.

Heading the delegation was Winston Tubman, a distinguished Liberian lawyer related to the family of the late William Tubman, one of Liberia's great presidents. In our discussions, we suggested that Doe consider moving up the presidential election scheduled for 1992 to 1991 in order to give Taylor and other presidential aspirants an opportunity to compete. Doe's response was legalistic. "Moving up the election would be unconstitutional."

While we were having discussions with Tubman, the rebels were advancing rapidly toward Monrovia, as the Liberian army fell back toward the capital city. Taylor was executing all Krahn prisoners, motivating the army to stop fighting and fall back to Monrovia. In addition to the army, civilians were fleeing from the rebels into Monrovia. By May 1990, the sanitary and health situations in Monrovia were deteriorating.

A new development in May was the decision by the Economic Community of West African States (ECOWAS) to send an intervention force to stop the fighting and establish conditions for a political solution. They assured Taylor that the intervention was not aimed at him and his rebels. He needed to stop fighting and compete for power politically. Within ECOWAS, Côte d'Ivoire and Burkina Faso, Taylor's ardent sponsors, bitterly opposed the decision to intervene in Liberia.

When the ECOWAS force came into Monrovia harbor, they were shelled by Taylor's artillery. It was clear that Taylor considered the ECOWAS force, known as ECOMOG, not as a neutral party but as his enemy. He decided to continue fighting in an effort to conquer Monrovia.

At this point, during May–June 1990, I decided to seek a solution by moving Doe out of Liberia and arranging for Taylor to take over the city peacefully. He had already taken over the rest of Liberia. I called President Eyadema of Togo with a request that he give Doe political asylum. Eyadema said he was not happy with the idea but would say yes if the United States requested it.

I asked Ambassador Bishop to talk to Doe about the need to evacuate, since there was no way he could stop Taylor by military means. I also spoke to Doe on the phone. I proposed sending a US military cargo plane to take him and his family to Togo. Doe said that he might be willing to leave, but he had some pre-departure demands. First, he wanted a full scholarship to Oxford University. Secondly, he wanted to take his entire stock of Coca-Cola on the aircraft along with his family and luggage. We told him that the Coca-Cola transport was approved, but we could not guarantee admission to Oxford.

Before we could execute the plan to take Doe out of Liberia, higher US authority canceled the project, and the war between Taylor on the one hand and ECOWAS and Doe on the other continued. In September 1990 a former Taylor fighter named Prince Johnson, who had broken with Taylor, assassinated Doe. Thus ended a political career that should never have started.

This first part of the Liberian civil war lasted until 1996, when the Nigerians brokered a truce. In an election in 1997, Charles Taylor was elected president. He had caused so much devastation during the fighting that the voters feared a recurrence of war if he were not elected. He became president more out of fear than of popularity.

Charles Taylor

When Taylor was leading his band of rebels deeper into Liberia toward Monrovia during 1990, he was clearly well equipped, thanks to Gaddafi, Burkina Faso, and Côte d'Ivoire. He had a satellite telephone that he used quite a lot, and he and I had several conversations through that channel. He tried his best to project a consistent image of a responsible freedom fighter. He was always reasonable in his speech. His main interest was not power, he insisted. All he wanted was democracy for Liberia.

Thinking about our own facilities in the Monrovia area, I tried to persuade him to avoid the destruction of infrastructure. I argued that in the event he took power, he would want to have what little infrastructure Liberia had for his own use. There was no reason to destroy what existed. He agreed wholeheartedly.

We learned from intelligence that Taylor was absolutely ruthless with any of his rebels who got out of line. He engaged in instant execution of anyone who failed to carry out orders or who retreated from the battle of the day. He had a falling out with one of his top lieutenants, Prince Johnson, who escaped to Monrovia before Taylor could shoot him. Johnson and his followers were determined to fight Taylor without aligning with Doe.

Around May 1990, the situation in Monrovia was so bad that I thought it best if Doe's military could be given an opening to escape to Sierra Leone. Monrovia is on a peninsula poking out into the Atlantic Ocean. Taylor had all escape routes blocked. I spoke to Taylor on his satellite phone and argued for his unblocking the road to Sierra Leone so that Doe's troops could get out. I argued that Doe's men knew they would be killed if captured. Therefore, they would fight in Monrovia to the death. If they were allowed to escape, they might take the opportunity to run away.

Taylor agreed and actually opened the corridor. But his new enemy Prince Johnson jumped in and blocked the corridor as part of his effort to fight Taylor. The situation in Monrovia continued to deteriorate.

In August 1990, I received an instruction from the White House to visit Liberia and the neighboring countries in order to demonstrate that the United States had not lost interest in the Liberia crisis. Criticism was building up in the Congress and the Liberian community that the US government had taken a passive attitude toward the Liberian civil war. As a matter of fact, we did move into a passive mode after the cancellation of my plan to evacuate President Doe a few months earlier in May. All of the action lay with ECOWAS and its ECOMOG intervention force on one side, and Charles Taylor and his National Patriotic Front of Liberia (NPFL) on the other. After his sensational assassination of Samuel Doe, Prince Johnson and his small band of fighters became less visible and less relevant, because they did not control any territory. The fighting continued with full force.

During my "show the flag" visit to the West African subregion in August 1990, my first stop was in Freetown, Sierra Leone, where President Momoh denounced President Houphouët-Boigny of Côte d'Ivoire as the man behind Liberia's agony. He was not wrong.

From Freetown, my executive assistant Karl Hoffman and I flew in a US Navy helicopter gunship to Monrovia, where we landed on the ambassador's lawn surrounded by a dozen fully armed US Marines in full battle dress. They were there to protect the Embassy from the nearby war. As I saw these American fighters, I had a brief recollection of my time in the US Army as an infantry platoon leader in Western Germany quite a few years earlier. I thought, "We could probably end this war with just these American marines." My time in Monrovia was spent mainly with the US embassy people and with Prince Johnson, who was willing to come to the Embassy. A meeting with President Doe was not possible due to the sniper fire in various parts of the city.

After Monrovia we flew to Abidjan in Côte d'Ivoire, where I met with President Houphouët-Boigny. He denied any involvement in the Liberian civil war. The key part of that trip was a meeting with Charles Taylor in his camp headquarters about ten miles inside Liberia from the Ivoirien border town of Man. I drove into Liberia from Man with our ambassador to Abidjan Kenneth Brown, Deputy Assistant Secretary of Defense James Woods, and Karl Hoffman.

As we approached Taylor's camp, we encountered young boys carrying assault weapons. They looked as if they were under the influence of drugs. This was our first experience with the phenomenon of boy soldiers that has become endemic to civil wars and surrogate wars in Africa. We were nervous, both on the way in and on the way out.

We found Taylor sitting in his tent in a throne-like chair. Behind him, hanging on a curtain, was a large photograph of President John F. Kennedy and his family. He was alone. If he had any close advisers there, they were not visible.

As he did on satellite phone conversations, Taylor demonstrated strong deference to high-level officials of the United States government. He was particularly impressed that a high official of the Pentagon was also visiting him.

Taylor wanted to know why the United States was so passive in view of Liberia's terrible situation. He said that if the United States sent in a battalion of US Marines, "We would all surrender." He seemed sincere about that. The United States was the natural father and mother of Liberia and could solve Liberia's problems. It was only a question of political will.

Since the fighting between his forces and those of ECOMOG appeared to be in a stalemate, with his fighters still over fifty miles from Monrovia, I asked Taylor if he would be willing to have a cease-fire with ECOMOG leading to negotiations. He said yes.

We left Taylor in his jungle headquarters with a distinct impression that this slight little guy, with a picture of President Kennedy behind him, was suffering from a "Napoleon complex." He saw himself as someone who had greatness thrust upon him. He would lead Liberia to wealth and prestige. Above all, he would be respected as a head of state.

From Abidjan, I informed Washington that Taylor said he was ready for a cease-fire with ECOMOG, to be followed by negotiations. The response was a slap on the wrist. "We told you not to take charge of the Liberia problem. Why are you negotiating again?" The war continued.

From August 1989 to my departure from office in April 1993, I followed orders and stayed away from the Liberia war, except for a few emergency evacuations of American citizens. The war continued until 1996, when the president of Nigeria persuaded Taylor to accept a cease-fire and an election that he was sure to win. Taylor won the election of 1997 with a totally destroyed infrastructure to worry about.

In 1998, I was in the consulting business. Officials of the Liberian international ship registry program approached me to ask if I would be willing to travel to Monrovia to advise President Taylor. I accepted. Based on my earlier conversations with him, I believed that he was ready for reconstruction and nation building. I signed on to a paid retainer for a three-month period.

In Monrovia, Taylor could not have been more respectful and courteous. He gave me full access to all government offices and spent a lot of time talking to me about his ambitions for Liberia. In the finance ministry, I met the deputy finance minister, who showed me his plan for a World Bank macroeconomic reform program, to be followed by an internationally financed reconstruction program. Having just completed a five-year contract with the World Bank, I read his draft program with great interest. I considered his work to be quite professional and a logical policy document.

In my final meeting with Taylor, I advised him that his minister's reform proposal under World Bank tutelage was the way to go as the first step in the rebuilding of Liberia. He thanked me for the advice, and we parted company, never to meet again.

Instead of taking the road of reform and rebuilding, Taylor decided to become a regional warlord, continuing his relationship with Gaddafi and Burkina Faso for the destabilization of Sierra Leone and Guinea (Conakry), both of which countries had sent troops to ECOMOG to fight him. He gave military support to the Revolutionary United Front (RUF) of Sierra Leone, financing arms purchases with "blood diamonds" pillaged from Sierra Leone's artisanal diamond diggers. Between 1999 and 2003, Taylor's actions plunged Liberia into a second civil war, which led to his downfall and indictment for war crimes by the Special International Court for Sierra Leone.

Having achieved the presidency of Liberia, why didn't Taylor stop when he was ahead and devote the rest of his career to the reconstruction of his country? He could have become a statesman and a hero to all Liberians. Did this little guy with a Napoleonic complex consider Liberia too small for someone with his talent? Did his ability to hold back the combined forces of Nigeria, Ghana, Sierra Leone, and Guinea go to his head? Was he trying to become the King of West Africa? Or was the Charles Taylor who had been accused of embezzling Liberian government money in 1987 just a chronic crook?

GROUP VI

The South Africans:
Keeping the Fires of Democracy Burning

Frederik W. de Klerk (left), former president of the Republic of South Africa, meets with Assistant Secretary of State Cohen in Cape Town in May 1990.
Credit: South African Presidency

The late South African president Nelson Mandela, recently released after twenty-seven years in prison, enters the State Department at the beginning of his first official visit to the United States in March 1990. Former assistant secretary of state Cohen is on Mandela's left.
Credit: State Department

CHAPTER 14

Nelson Mandela and F. W. de Klerk

"At the end of the day, we are all Christians"

Historical Note

In post-colonial Africa, the Republic of South Africa has been, and continues to be, a special case. Having achieved independence as a British Dominion in 1910, South Africa was one of only three African countries independent of colonial rule at the end of the Second World War. The other two were Liberia and Ethiopia. But applying the term "independent" to South Africa was disingenuous. In reality, between 1910 and 1990, South Africa was an independent country that encompassed an internal colonial system. Fifteen percent of the population, white people of European (British and Dutch) extraction, exercised absolute rule over 85 percent of the people designated as "non-white." Starting in 1948, the white population of South Africa imposed a ruthless form of racial segregation they called *apartheid*—the Afrikaner word for a society that was determined to divide all of the nonwhite racial groups into separate independent impoverished mini states.

Because the white government of South Africa had a modern, sophisticated administration, the international community tended to ignore the horrible racial injustices being perpetrated inside the country. South Africa was a strong international trading partner with a high-quality diplomatic service and a good internal environment for investors. It was a country viewed as being in an advanced state of economic development compared to the rest of sub-Saharan Africa, which was in an embryonic state of development.

The South African system remained internally and internationally viable until the early 1980s, when the younger generation of black youth, seeing only a bleak future, began to rebel against the racial repression with increasing militancy. As street demonstrations grew more and more violent, the white government's response grew more and more lethal. With advanced global communications, the horrors of racial conflict drew the attention of the international community. In the United States the negative reaction was nearly universal. Most American communities at all levels, and among all ethnic groups, reacted strongly to what was going on in South Africa. The US political system, through the Congress, took notice and enacted severe economic sanctions against South Africa to get the white government's attention. In 1987, President Reagan had the creative idea of sending an African American career diplomat, Edward Perkins, as ambassador to South Africa, with the instruction to "shake those people up." Thus began a transitional process that led to the ending of political repression in 1990 and the beginning of majority rule in 1994.

In 1988, South Africa entered a period of political transition designed to bring an end to a system that could not remain viable in an increasingly globalized world. This transition brought to the forefront two political leaders, who created a new political dispensation—one that was democratic, multiracial, tolerant, and conciliatory—different from any other on the African continent. I got to know these two leaders, Nelson Mandela and F. W. de Klerk, during the transition and was inspired by their vision and strength. Unlike the other African leaders described in this treatise, Mandela and de Klerk were strongmen in their own way—in their determination to get rid of the old and give rise to a new South Africa that would lead the rest of Africa to modernization. What was interesting to me was to determine why their story was so different from the rest of Africa's strong leaders.

My first encounter with F. W. de Klerk took place in 1989, when he was minister of education. Our private conversation took place in his hotel suite on the seafront in Durban, the major port city and beach resort on South Africa's Indian Ocean coast. He was in the midst of a presidential election campaign that looked very favorable to him. Indeed, he spoke to me with the confidence of a future president.

De Klerk told me that he was born into apartheid, raised under apartheid, and had become an enthusiastic leader of the apartheid movement. Nevertheless, he had reached the conclusion that there was no place for apartheid in a modern South Africa. His first grandson had just been born. Unless apartheid was abolished, he said, there would be no future for his grandson in South Africa, where his ancestors had lived for over two hundred years.

Needless to say, I was knocked for a loop, although white South African business travelers had been telling us for over a year that de Klerk was coming and would be making important changes. I had not anticipated the type of revolutionary changes he envisioned.

De Klerk said that he planned to release Mandela and the other political prisoners. He also planned to legalize all of the African political parties, including the ANC and the Communist Party. Negotiations would then begin for a majority rule dispensation.

The only way South Africa could move into the modern globalized world, de Klerk said, would be to totally integrate the black community into the South African economy; and the only way to accomplish that would be to accord the black population full political rights.

De Klerk did not apologize for apartheid. He did not say that it was wrong and, therefore, immoral. He had believed in it for a long time, and then no longer did. Both he and Nelson Mandela were thereby joined at the hip as hardheaded politicians working to make South Africa live up to its vast potential.

I left that meeting wondering if De Klerk could pull it off. His main electoral support base, the Afrikaner population, did not demonstrate the same interest in change that animated him. But I did see some signs of change in the younger generation. Working on the negotiations to persuade South Africa to bring its UN mandate, Namibia, to independence, I noted that young white South African men were demonstrating against the military conscription that was taking them to fight a guerrilla war in Namibia against nationalist insurgents. If the younger generation was losing the will to maintain power by sheer force, maybe their parents were thinking differently.

***

I saw some interesting changes of attitude within the black leadership, too. In early 1987, I had just begun my assignment as senior director for Africa on the National Security Council staff and special assistant to President Ronald Reagan. During a routine orientation visit to South Africa, the American embassy suggested that I visit the African township of Soweto, just outside of Johannesburg. Soweto was the center of black political debate and action planning.

I started with a visit to the home of Albertina Sisulu, the wife of Mandela's prison mate of twenty-five years, Walter Sisulu. Albertina, a leading anti-apartheid militant in her own right, was confined to her home under house arrest. During our discussion over tea, I said that we were hearing from business sources that the white political leadership was thinking about ending apartheid and moving toward majority rule. But there was fear in the white community about the unknown consequences of such a change, after so many years of harsh repression of the black population.

Albertina laughed and said, "Why should they worry? We are all Christians." That response really flicked a light bulb on in my head. As de Klerk [had] predicted at our meeting the previous August, Nelson Mandela was released from political prison in February 1990. His charisma and popularity were so great that he could have become the "strongman" of the new majority-ruled South Africa. Apart from his determination to seek reconciliation rather than revenge, his guiding political outlook was loyalty to the African National Congress. Unlike other African leaders who paid lip service to the development of "consensus" within the ruling party, Mandela actually practiced it. He could have been the dictatorial strongman, but it was not in his political nature.

I first met Mandela in Windhoek, Namibia, in March 1990 on the occasion of the Namibia independence celebrations, only a month after his liberation from custody. He was there as the leader of the South African delegation. I was a member of the official United States delegation led by Secretary of State James Baker. Baker and I called on Mandela at his villa.

Baker told Mandela that he was planning to visit Cape Town, Johannesburg, and Pretoria for about a week after the Namibia events. Mandela became quite agitated and demanded that Baker not go to South Africa. Mandela argued that South Africa was still under apartheid rule. Negotiations for a democratic, majority rule dispensation still had a long way to go. Mandela said that the white political leadership could not be trusted. His release could have been purely cosmetic to deceive international public opinion. He told Baker that a visit by the American secretary of state would confer premature legitimacy on the illegal regime of F. W. de Klerk. Baker replied that de Klerk's new regime needed encouragement to move forward with majority rule, and he was determined to make the visit. The meeting ended cordially, but there was tension in the atmosphere.

I next saw Mandela in Washington in June 1990 after he accepted President Bush's invitation to make an official visit. By that time, he was co-president of South Africa with de Klerk. He traveled with Thabo Mbeki, the vice president of the African National Congress, who led the party in exile, based in Lusaka, Zambia.

The first event during his three-day official visit was a luncheon at the State Department hosted by Secretary of State Baker. I waited for him at the diplomatic entrance of the State Department. As he got out of the car, Mandela shook my hand and said, "Mr. Cohen, now that I see you, I know that everything will be OK." That was my first experience with Mandela's legendary charm.

Secretary Baker and President Bush made Mandela's visit into a very big occasion. Mandela was received with full honors on the White House lawn. Any bitterness that arose during the March argument with Baker dissipated at that point. In the discussions during the luncheon and White House meeting, Mandela and Mbeke were consumed with the long negotiations that awaited them in the writing of a new constitution.

After the visit, Baker asked for my prognosis about the negotiations. I told him that the negotiations had to be difficult because so much was at stake and because there was so much mistrust after decades of racial oppression. Baker asked me if the United States could have a role as a mediator. I replied that the United States had the trust of both sides, despite our late entry into the anti-apartheid struggle. Baker had seen for himself that the black militants he spoke to during his visit to South Africa considered the United States an unbiased player. I suggested that we give it a try.

Two weeks later, President Bush gave the annual White House barbeque for the diplomatic corps. During the party, he, Secretary Baker, and I talked to the South African ambassador about the idea of our providing mediation services. A few weeks later we received a reply delivered through our ambassador, William Swing, in Pretoria. Both sides in the negotiations had discussed the idea of US mediation, and had reached the conclusion that the political transition from apartheid to democracy was a matter for South Africans alone. They would do without a mediator, thank you very much.

Mandela's overall conciliatory outlook did not mean that he was soft and malleable. On the contrary, he took a realistic and tough view of South African and international politics. One of the black South African politicians most detested by the ANC was Mangosuthu Buthelezi, the founder and president of the Inkatha Freedom Party in Natal Province. The ANC considered Buthelezi a "sellout to apartheid" because he served as prime minister of a geographic entity designated to become an independent Bantustan. These were to be the independent nations to which all black peoples would belong, leaving the whites the only legitimate South Africans, owning the wealthiest and most productive lands.

Mandela remained loyal to Buthelezi, because Buthelezi resisted the apartheid government's pressure to bring his Bantustan to independence so long as Mandela and the other political detainees remained in prison. Mandela did not forget Buthelezi's loyalty, and he made sure that the ANC did not take revenge. Indeed, after majority rule, Buthelezi was named minister of interior.

Muammar Gaddafi was a major supporter of the ANC prior to the arrival of freedom. When Mandela made his first trip abroad in 1990, his first stop was Libya, much to the chagrin of the Americans and others. Above all, Mandela was loyal.

In one of my many conversations with Mandela in his Johannesburg home, I suggested that in view of the size and complexity of South Africa, the constitution should be written to provide for a decentralized federal system, like the United States. The concept was anathema to most of the ANC leadership, who envisioned a highly centralized state in the Marxist-Leninist model. When I suggested decentralization, Mandela did not demur. He said that he knew the ANC leadership in most of the outlying areas, and they told him that they did not necessarily trust those guys in ANC headquarters in Johannesburg to do what was right for them. In the end, the South African constitution indeed created decentralized provinces, with elected governors. With all but one province controlled by ANC politicians, South Africa looks like a highly centralized country; but with Western Cape Province under the control of an opposition party, and very well governed, it is clear that federalism has a future.

I witnessed Mandela's ability to be tough and stubborn when he considered it expedient. During the four years of negotiations, he walked out a few times to express disgust with the white negotiators. At one tense point, white extremists were stirring up ethnic violence in the black townships in order to sabotage the discussions. Mandela walked out of the talks and said they would not resume until the violence stopped. This required that I travel to South Africa. I held a press conference to say that the only way to deal with political violence was to ignore it and persevere with the negotiations. Giving violence credibility would only invite more violence. Mandela got the point and returned to the negotiating table. But he demonstrated that when it came to the future of his country he was not "Mr. Nice Guy."

An irony of the two parties' decision not to invite the United States to be a mediator was their regular *ad hoc* recourse to successive American ambassadors, William Swing and Princeton Lyman, each time there was an impasse. In substance, the United States was the mediator, but only when the negotiations became stalled. I called the process an "invisible American mediation."

My last opportunity to talk to Mandela took place in 1995. Majority rule was in place, and he was the sole president. His vice president, Thabo Mbeki, was the effective administrator of government. I met Mandela then at a conference organized by the Newseum, the American organization that defends the freedom of the press. I was no longer in government. He was the principal speaker, and I was invited to be in the audience. As I sat down about ten rows from the podium, Mandela spotted me. He got up and walked all the way to my seat to shake my hand. I could not have been more proud.

***

South Africa's experience was different from that of the other African colonialized nations. After escaping from British rule in the early part of the twentieth century, South Africa entered into a long period of internal colonialism where 15 percent of the population exercised total control over the other 85 percent. To a certain extent, the experiences did not look that different to the average black person living under European colonial rule or white South African internal colonial rule. If that is the case, why is the South African leadership's legacy of democracy, rule of law, and ethnic tolerance so different from most of the African continent?

I have spoken to a wide variety of South Africans, especially those in Mandela's and de Klerk's generation, and reached the conclusion that South Africa is different because of its long history of exposure to, and absorption of, Christianity. Over three centuries, Christianity had become more deeply ingrained in the different ethnic groups of South Africa than anywhere else in Africa. I believe this explains why white South Africa and Black South Africa were able to come together to establish a new dispensation for their country, despite the horrible events of the past. This is pure hypothesizing, based on conversations rather than research, but I believe in it sincerely.

My hope is that South Africa will continue to be a moral beacon for the rest of Africa. For this reason, I am pleased to see a growing South African presence in the rest of Africa through private sector investments.

CONCLUSIONS

CHAPTER 15

The Legacy of Africa's First Leadership Generation and the US Response

The African leaders portrayed in this volume were typical of their generation. Their outlooks were somewhat contradictory. They rejected colonial-era institutions, yet they adopted some colonial-era socioeconomic theories.

The newly independent African nations of the early 1960s rejected Western multiparty democracy and all of the trappings of open societies. Relying on the African tradition of consensus building to settle disputes, the early leaders adopted the "African one-party state." Within this all-encompassing monolith, all issues would be discussed, and policies would be developed through consensus.

Since adversarial conflict, so prevalent within Western democracies, was to be avoided at all cost, all institutions of civil society had to be incorporated into the "African one-party state." While everyone inside the party was building consensus, it was unacceptable for independent media or independent organizations to be out there sniping away at both the process and the policies. Thus, all media were either state-owned or attached to the ruling party. Almost all civil society organizations were party organizations. Every single party had built-in youth, women's, workers, and other mass organizations. Independent voices were in short supply.

On the economic side, the first generation of African leaders was caught up in the West European fascination with 1960s Marxist Socialism. The early leaders' role models were the French Socialist Party and the British Labour Party. Most educated people under the age of forty in those days believed in socialist principles, and many African leaders spent their under-forty years in France and Britain absorbing socialist ideology. Almost all of the leaders of newly independent African nations in the 1960s adopted the same two-pronged approach to governance: the "African one-party state" and "African socialism." Implementation varied according to cultural differences, but the basic approach was similar throughout Africa.

The results of the early policies of the first generation of African leaders were generally not happy ones for their populations. The one-party state descended into corruption and varying degrees of authoritarian rule. In many countries, dissident voices violated the consensus rules and had to be silenced. Political prisoners were commonplace. The single-party bureaucracies swelled with careerists who constituted a parallel government, with private access to state resources. They had a stake in maintaining the single party in power, come what may.

On the economic side, the socialist principles adopted from UK and French mentors resulted in mass nationalizations of private enterprises, including banks, insurance companies, plantations, downstream oil entities, and light manufacturing. Unlike their counterparts in France and the UK, the African state managers of the nationalized enterprises did not assign high priorities to profit making and the reinvestment of profits for growth. On the contrary, their priorities were the expansion of employment for party and ethnic faithful and the establishment of sources of funding for maintaining party loyalties among various constituencies, with a special emphasis on the security forces.

It was not long before government-owned enterprises became loss making, thereby requiring government subsidies. This caused money to be taken away from essential government services, including healthcare, education, and infrastructure maintenance. The deterioration of services caused further disinvestment by enterprises that had not been nationalized and totally discouraged new investors. A vicious cycle ensued that caused most African countries to suffer from negative growth for over two decades.

By the mid-1980s, the United States and the other major donors to African development had become thoroughly disillusioned by the growth of authoritarian governance and the mismanagement of African economies. The World Bank and the International Monetary Fund were called in to force-feed economic reform programs, which succeeded over a decade in reversing economic decline in most of the countries.

At the same time, a new generation of educated Africans started to demand a political opening for free expression and democratic transition. This resulted in a decline of authoritarian governance, including the closing of political prisons, the rise of independent media, and the slow building of opposition political parties. Of equal significance has been the slow acceptance of private enterprise, created by indigenous investors, as partners in development rather than as threats to the power structure.

As of early 2015, Africa was making progress on both the political and economic fronts. Most governments were tolerating opposition political parties, and were holding "free and fair" elections. But in only a few countries were the ruling political families and parties willing to take the risk of losing an election. It was impossible to say that more than a handful of countries had entered a transition to irreversible democracy.

While enjoying significant economic growth since the year 2000, due mainly to a worldwide boom in commodity prices, there were still no African countries in early 2014 that could claim sustainable economic development. The absence of the rule of law in most of the countries, as well as the pervasive corruption of bureaucracies at all levels, made even the most willing indigenous investors still reluctant to take risks. The major exceptions are the investors closely tied to the ruling families and ruling parties.

On the basis of my extended conversations with the leaders described in this volume, as well as less extensive conversations with most of the others in the first generation, what conclusions can I draw about Africa's slow progress toward modernization?

The African leaders whom I knew well wanted to advance the welfare of their populations, albeit in their own way. But they had a cultural block in the sense that they saw the masses as "children" who needed parental guidance. The idea of taking the time and expending resources to find out what the people aspire to at their own levels was unthinkable. The people had to be directed, top down. It was paternalism on steroids. In my experience, the only people who tried to find out what the African rural peasants wanted to achieve were the foreign aid workers, especially the American Peace Corps volunteers, and charitable organizations such as Catholic Relief.

President Mobutu's remark to me about the hopelessness of the Congolese people expressed crudely what many of the first generation leaders felt in their hearts. The African interpretation of "socialism" fit very well into this view of African populations. The state will be responsible for everything. As the African father wanted to exercise total parental control over his children, even into early adulthood, the African state exercised total control over the citizen-children of the nation.

A good example of this outlook took place in Tanzania under the presidency of Julius Nyerere, one of the most revered of the African founding fathers. (I did not write about him because I did not know him personally.) He was advised by some of his educated associates that rural development would not be possible as long as the Tanzanian farmers lived in such small villages with such small populations. Economies of scale were needed. So, Nyerere implemented a policy of enforced relocation to larger villages. Small villages would be regrouped into larger entities. The plan did not work, because the peasants were not consulted and because the concept violated cultural norms. The same policy was tried and failed in Ethiopia.

Secondly, the first African leaders were prisoners of cultural and ethnic inhibitors. Ethnic pressures made it difficult for them to diversify the political process. President Houphouët-Boigny had to keep his own Baule ethnic group on top and thus found it difficult to tap the talents of other groups. President Senghor knew that the two major Muslim brotherhoods controlled hundreds of thousands of votes. He needed to make sure they were happy, and they were happy with the ultraconservative status quo. President Bongo knew that the most intellectually advanced ethnic group in Gabon was the Fang, who were also in the majority. He could not allow their leaders to win power, because he knew that they would overwhelm the other ethnic groups. Hence, he ruled as a minority president for four decades until his death. The great talent and entrepreneurship of the Fang were eclipsed, and the country suffered.

Thirdly, the first generation of African rulers liked the comfortable attractions of the international scene. Going to conferences and acting as mediators were far more interesting activities than coping with rural poverty. Senghor saw himself as an important statesman who could operate in the francophone world, the African world, and the Islamic world. Houphouët-Boigny believed that all of the countries on Côte d'Ivoire's borders were subject to his strong influence, and he exercised that influence, sometimes with disastrous impact. Bongo was an effective regional mediator, but an ineffective president at home. Kaunda was happiest dealing with liberation movements and conflict resolution in southern Africa. Dealing with external problems was always easier and more comfortable than intractable internal issues.

Fourth, the first generation African leaders were obsessed with their images at home. It seems as if the desire to be loved by their peoples was in direct proportion to the degree of their absolute power. I believe that absolute power does not instill a sense of security. I believe that the absolute rulers of Africa, especially those of the first generation, thought about the security of their power as their first priority when they got up in the morning. The next coup was never out of mind. The few that have accepted free and fair elections, as well as the risk of losing the next election, are the ones with the greatest feeling of day-to-day security, in my view. The strongmen of Africa are so worried about their security that they must pay a great deal of attention to their public images.

Fifth, the first generation leadership deserves credit for a significant development—most Africans consider themselves citizens of their countries and have a sense of nationhood. In the Democratic Republic of the Congo, where Mobutu reigned as the "Paramount Chief" for thirty-one years, there is a general sentiment of being a Congolese person, living in the Congolese Republic. Considering the vast size of the DRC and the vast diversity of languages and ethnic nations, the widespread feeling of Congolese nationhood is a tribute to Mobutu. This is true, as well, in most of the independent African nations, divided as some of them are by ethnic animosities. Pride in being a citizen of an African nation is widespread in Africa, even if the average quality of life in many of those nations has not grown much since independence.

Sixth, the experience of the first generation of African leadership demonstrates that the persons who led the struggle for freedom did not necessarily make the best persons to lead and govern independent nations. Mugabe, Kaunda, Senghor, and Kabila were good examples of this phenomenon.

Finally, the first generation of African leadership failed to deal with Africa's dirty little secret, the widespread use of illegitimate surrogate wars. Fifty years after the independence of most African nations, illegitimate surrogate wars continue to be the instruments African governments employ in seeking to destabilize their neighbors.

- Rwanda and Uganda sponsored Congolese surrogates to overthrow Mobutu in 1996.
- Côte d'Ivoire and Burkina Faso sponsored Liberian surrogates to overthrow Samuel Doe in 1990.
- Rwanda and Uganda sponsored a second set of Congolese surrogates in a failed attempt to overthrow Kabila in 1998.
- Zambia and South Africa supported Jonas Savimbi in his attempt to undermine the government of Angola between 1975 and 1992.
- Burkina Faso sponsored Côte d'Ivoire surrogates in a successful effort to destabilize the government of Laurent Gbagbo during 2005–2011.

While the African Union will instantly expel any government that comes to power through a military coup, the African Union continues to ignore the illegitimate surrogate wars that are so devastating to life and property.

What are the prospects for the new generation of African leadership that has come to power since 1995? Can the new leaders overcome the cultural inhibitors, ethnic pressures, and fears of globalization that beset their elders? The jury is still out, but there are promising signs among some of the younger leaders who understand technology, who listen to the people, and who wake up in the morning determined to do good. The international community needs to identify these promising leaders and concentrate their development assistance on helping them succeed.

Where do the current black political leaders of South Africa fit into the overall sociopolitical matrix of the African continent? Two decades after the beginning of black majority rule, South Africa continues to be the beacon of democracy. We are now seeing more and more of the new generation of African leaders looking to South Africa as a role model for tolerance and fairness.

What about United States policy toward Africa during the half century since the beginning of the independence wave?

Having pushed the European powers to move toward liberating their African colonies expeditiously, the United States has consistently taken a positive view of Africa's ambitions for sustained economic development. The United States has concentrated its policies toward the continent on support for economic development. Strategic and national security interests have never been significant US priorities in Africa, even during the height of the Cold War.

At the same time, the United States has been reluctant to criticize Africa's self-destructive policies, leaving the blunt talk to the World Bank and the International Monetary Fund. There has always been a sentiment in Washington that we should allow the Africans to feel good about their independence and that we are not about to act as "neocolonials."

President Barack Obama appears more inclined than his predecessors toward "tough love" with respect to Africa. As an American of African descent, he feels he can talk openly about corruption and human rights abuses. He can get away with telling the Africans to face reality and move toward good governance before their growing populations of unemployed youth become explosive. Some of the second and third generations of African leaders appear to be taking him seriously. Thus, there are grounds for optimism in Africa in the second decade of the twenty-first century.

Index

CPSIA information can be obtained
at www.ICGtesting.com
Printed in the USA
LVHW030805220122
708923LV00004B/523